Usborne
Thousands
of
Searches

Contents

Part One

The Dinosaur Search

This part of the book is all about dinosaurs and the world they lived in. It's also an exciting puzzle. If you look hard at the pictures, you'll be able to spot hundreds of dinosaurs and the creatures that lived at the same time as them. You can see below how the puzzles work.

The writing next to each little picture tells you the name of the animal or plant and how many you can find in the big picture.

Look very carefully to count all the dinosaurs in the distance.

This Protoceratops is hatching, but it still counts.

Although this lizard is coming out of the big picture, you should still count it.

These young dinosaurs also count.

You can only see part of this Protoceratops, but it still counts.

There are about 100 animals to spot in each picture. If you get stuck, the answers are on pages 28–31. Not all the animals are dinosaurs, only the ones with a symbol next to them like the one on the right. In real life there wouldn't have been this many animals in one place at the same time.

Dinosaur symbol

Shallow seas

Over 400 million years ago, the Silurian seas were full of strange creatures. Many of these have died out, but some, such as sponges and jellyfish, can still be found in the oceans today.

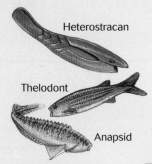

Heterostracan

Thelodont

Anapsid

These fish sucked food and water through their mouths. Find seven of each type.

Jellyfish looked much the same as they do now. Spot five.

Brachiopods were animals with fleshy stalks which they buried in the sand. Find 14.

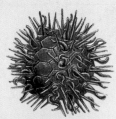

Sea urchins crawled slowly across the sea floor. Spot eight.

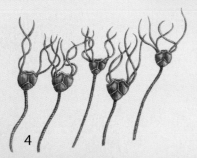

Sea-lilies were animals, not plants. They caught food with their wavy arms. Spot 15.

Marine snails could hide inside their shells. Find 14.

Nostolepis was one of the first fish to have jaws and teeth. Spot 13.

4

Osteostracan fish had bony shields covering their heads. Spot nine.

Cephalopods were decorated with beautiful patterns. Spot four of each of these.

Silurian starfish didn't look the same as modern starfish. Spot 11.

Graptolites were made up of lots of small animals joined together. Find two.

Shrimps like the one above darted through the shallow water. Find 14.

Trilobites walked along the sea floor, looking for food. Spot 12.

Sponges were animals with soft, fleshy bodies. Spot five.

This giant Eurypterid was a fierce hunter. Can you spot another one?

5

Living on the land

400 million years ago, fish with lungs for breathing air began to crawl out of the water. These fish slowly changed over millions of years, until they had legs for walking and could live on land.

Bothriolepis used its jointed fins to walk along the bottom of lakes. Spot five.

Clubmosses had branching stems covered with tiny, scaly leaves. Find nine plants.

Scientists think Aglaophyton was one of the first plants to grow on land. Spot six.

These are Ichthyostega eggs. Spot four groups.

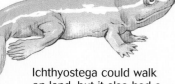

Ichthyostega could walk on land, but it also had a fish-like tail. Spot four.

Groenlandaspis was a fish with bony plates to protect its head. Find five.

Shark-like Ctenacanthus glided through the water in search of prey. Spot one.

Ichthyostegopsis used its flipper-like legs to swim after fish. Find two.

Panderichthys had four fins that looked like arms and legs. Can you find three?

You can still see horsetail plants in wet and marshy places. Spot 16.

Water beetles looked the same as they do today. Find nine.

These woodlice were one of the first animals to live on land. Spot ten.

Shrimps fed on tiny bits of food which floated in the water. Can you find 15?

Acanthostega had gills like a fish, for breathing underwater. Spot seven.

Mimia fishes were about the size of your thumb. Spot 18.

Eusthenopteron used its fins to prop itself up on the banks of lakes and rivers. Spot three.

Giant insects

In the steamy Carboniferous swamps, gigantic insects zoomed through the air, while venomous bugs crawled through the thick, tangled undergrowth.

Pholidogaster was a strong swimmer and a fierce hunter. Spot two.

Meganeura had a wingspan that was as long as a human's arm. Spot four.

Cockroaches had flat bodies. They could squeeze under things to hide. Spot 15.

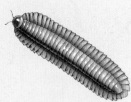

The centipede Arthropleura sometimes grew up to 2m (6½ft) long. Find six.

The word Hylonomus means "forest mouse". Spot seven.

Gephyrostegus had sharp teeth for crunching up insects. Spot six.

Giant scorpions could kill other animals by stinging them. Find three.

Archaeothyris had strong jaws which helped it to kill its prey. Find three.

The first snails appeared on land at this time. Before, they had lived underwater. Spot ten.

Lizard-like Microsaurs lived on land but laid their eggs in water. Spot 11.

Ophiderpeton had no arms or legs, and looked like an eel. Can you spot five?

Spiders spun simple webs to catch their prey. Find seven.

Westlothiana was a reptile. It laid eggs with hard shells and lived on dry land. Spot ten.

Giant millipedes fed on rotting leaves. Spot five.

Eogyrinus was the size of a crocodile. It snapped up fish in its powerful jaws. Find four.

Gerrothorax lay at the bottom of rivers, waiting to catch passing fish. Spot one.

9

Rocky landscape

During this time, lots of animals appeared that could live on land. The most striking of these had huge sails on their backs. Many of these creatures died out before the arrival of the dinosaurs.

Yougina had strong, sharp teeth for cracking open snail shells. Spot three.

Pareiasaurus grew as big as a hippopotamus. Spot three.

Protorosaurus reared up on its back legs to catch insects to eat. Find four.

Sphenacodon had a ridge on its back. Spot six.

Seymouria couldn't move fast on land. It spent most of its time in water. Spot three.

Scientists know Sauroctonus was a meat-eater, because its teeth were long and sharp. Find four.

Diadectes had legs which stuck out on either side of its body, just like a modern lizard. Spot seven.

Edaphosaurus warmed itself up by letting the Sun heat the blood in a sail on its back. Can you spot 11?

Moschops was the size of a cow. Can you find four?

Cacops had a big head compared to the size of its body. Spot nine.

Long bones sticking out from Dimetrodon's spine held up a sail on its back. Find five.

Eryops was a distant relative of modern frogs. Spot two.

Anteosaurus bit chunks of flesh off its prey, then swallowed them whole. Spot two.

Casea had teeth all over the roof of its mouth, to crush up plants. Find four.

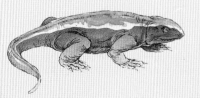

Scutosaurus had thick skin, and spikes sticking out of its cheeks. Spot three.

Bradysaurus had a neck frill at the back of its skull. Find one.

The first dinosaurs

About 225 million years ago, the first dinosaurs appeared. There are six different kinds of dinosaurs to spot here, along with some of the other strange creatures that lived at the same time.

Kuehneosaurus had thin sails of skin, which it used to glide from tree to tree. Spot four.

Although Cynognathus looked a little like a dog, it had scaly skin. Spot one.

Terrestrisuchus was about the size of a squirrel. Spot eight.

The dinosaur Staurikosaurus probably hunted in packs. Can you find seven?

The dinosaur Plateosaurus could rear up on its back legs. Find six.

Rutiodon had nostrils on the top of its head, between its eyes. Find two.

Ticinosuchus had strong, long legs so it could move very quickly. Spot five.

Saltopus, a dinosaur, scampered over rocks searching for lizards to eat. Can you find ten?

Syntarsus had sharp eyes and great speed to help it catch its prey. Spot four.

Peteinosaurus was one of the first flying lizards. Find three.

Placerias lived in herds and roamed long distances in search of food. Spot ten.

Desmatosuchus had long spikes sticking out from its shoulders. Spot three.

The dinosaur Coelophysis was a skilful hunter. Find seven.

Anchisaurus was one of the first dinosaurs. It was 2.5m (8ft) long. Spot five.

Stagonolepis may have dug for roots with its snout. Can you spot four?

Thrinaxodon had whiskers on its face and a furry body. Find five.

In the forest

The largest dinosaurs ever to walk the Earth lived at this time. Growing to enormous sizes, these giant creatures fed on the lush trees and plants which grew in the warm, wet climate.

Brachiosaurus' nostrils were on the top of a bump on its head. Spot one.

Pterodactylus snapped insects out of the air as it flew. Spot ten.

Apatosaurus swallowed leaves whole because it could not chew. Spot five.

Camptosaurus could run on its back legs if it was chased. Find two.

Fierce meat-eater Ceratosaurus had over 70 saw-edged fangs. Spot one.

Compsognathus is one of the smallest known dinosaurs. It was no bigger than a cat. Find eight.

Camarasaurus ate leaves from the lower tree branches. Spot three.

Diplodocus was as long as three buses parked end to end. Can you spot six?

Dryosaurus may have lived in herds like modern deer. Spot 17.

Archaeopteryx was probably the first bird. It flew from tree to tree. Find three.

Kentrosaurus had large spines on its back and tail. Spot one.

Scaphognathus had excellent eyesight. Can you find two?

Allosaurus had bony ridges above its eyes. Spot three.

Ornitholestes used its sharp claws to grab lizards and other small animals. Spot three.

Coelurus had long legs and could run fast to catch its prey. Spot two.

The bony plates on Stegosaurus' back may have absorbed heat from the Sun. Find two.

In the ocean

While dinosaurs roamed the land in Jurassic times, huge reptiles swam through the vast oceans.

There are 87 creatures to spot on these two pages. How many can you find?

Pleurosaurus had a long body and an even longer tail. Can you spot four?

Brittle stars still live in today's oceans. They have five long arms. Spot eight.

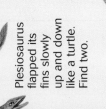

Plesiosaurus flapped its fins slowly up and down like a turtle. Find two.

Sharks sank to the bottom of the ocean if they didn't keep swimming. Spot six.

Liopleurodon ate other large sea creatures such as Ichthyosaurs. Spot one.

Pleurosternon needed to go up to the surface to breathe. Can you spot two?

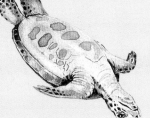

Rhomaleosaurus was as big as a modern killer whale, and just as fierce. Spot two.

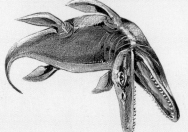

King crabs walked along the ocean floor. Spot three.

Belemnites had suckers on their arms. Spot ten.

Ichthyosaurus could swim fast by moving its powerful tail. Spot four.

Crocodile-like Geosaurus had paddle-shaped flippers. Find two.

Eurhinosaurus had a very long top jaw with lots of sharp teeth. Spot three.

Ammonites used their long tentacles to catch food. Find 14.

Banjo fish used their wing-like fins to glide through the water. Spot five.

There were many different kinds of fish. Spot ten of each of these.

Teleosaurus swam with snake-like movements. Spot one.

17

Dusty desert

The dinosaurs that lived in desert areas of what is now Mongolia and China suffered terrible dust storms. Some choked to death, while others were buried alive in sand dunes.

Oviraptor built nests for their eggs and sat on them until they hatched. Spot 12.

Psittacosaurus had a bony beak like a parrot's. Find four adults and six young.

Tarbosaurus ran after its prey with powerful bursts of speed. Can you find one?

Saurolophus had a bony spike on top of its head. Spot four.

These lizards fed on dinosaur eggs. Find eight.

If Pinacosaurus was attacked, it used the club on its tail as a weapon. Spot two.

18

Protoceratops laid its eggs in nests in the sand. Find five.

Protoceratops' nest

Microceratops was about the size of a rabbit. Spot 15.

Saurornithoides had large eyes and may have been able to see in the dark. Find ten.

Small mammals ran through the undergrowth catching insects to eat. Spot five.

Bactrosaurus had hundreds of teeth for chewing tough leaves. Spot seven.

Velociraptor means "speedy killer". It was a vicious meat-eater. Spot six.

Gallimimus ran on its back legs like an ostrich, but it didn't have any feathers. Find 11.

Avimimus was unusual, because it had feathers on its body. Spot seven.

Homalocephale had a thick skull with knobs on the sides. Spot three.

19

The last dinosaurs

During the late Cretaceous Period, there were more types of dinosaurs than at any other point in history. But then, about 64 million years ago, the dinosaurs suddenly died out.

Parasaurolophus used a tube on its head to make trumpet-like noises. Spot six.

Styracosaurus looked very fierce, but it only ate plants. Can you spot one?

Corythosaurus had a crest-like helmet on its head. Spot three.

Edmontosaurus lived in groups for protection against predators. Spot eight.

Panoplosaurus had spikes on its sides, but its belly was unprotected. Find two.

Pachycephalosaurus males had head-butting contests. Can you find five?

Triceratops weighed twice as much as an elephant. Spot four adults and two young.

Euoplocephalus may have swung the club on the end of its tail at attackers. Find three.

Ferocious hunter Tyrannosaurus was taller than a modern giraffe. Spot one.

Stenonychosaurus may have been clever, because it had a big brain. Find seven.

Ichythornis was one of the first birds. Find six.

Struthiomimus looked like an ostrich, but with no feathers. Spot nine.

Stegoceras belonged to a group of dinosaurs called dome heads. Spot seven.

Pentaceratops had a neck frill which reached halfway down its back. Spot three.

Nodosaurus means "lumpy reptile". Spot two.

Dromaeosaurus killed larger dinosaurs by hunting in packs. Spot 12.

Woodland mammals

When the dinosaurs died out, mammals took their place. Mammals are warm-blooded animals. They have fur or hair, give birth to babies and feed them with milk.

Tetonis gripped onto branches with its strong hands and feet. Spot five.

These bats hunted insects at night and slept during the day. Spot five.

Hyrachus was about the size of a pig. It could run very fast. Spot six.

Uintatherium was as large as a rhino, with six bony lumps on its head. Spot one.

Smilodectes used its long tail for balance as it climbed trees. Spot four.

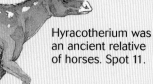

Hyracotherium was an ancient relative of horses. Spot 11.

Coryphodon means "curved tusks". It may have used them to defend itself. Spot three.

Mesonyx had teeth like a dog, but hooves instead of paws. Find three.

Diatryma was a giant bird. It stood 2m (6½ft) tall. Spot two.

Notharctus looked a little like a monkey. Spot seven.

Leptictidium was an omnivore, which means it ate plants and animals. Spot eight.

Oxyaena was a cat-like hunter that crept up on its prey. Spot two.

Venomous snakes curled around branches to sleep. Spot three.

Moeritherium probably lived in and around water. Spot one.

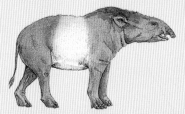

Eomanis had no teeth. It used its long tongue to lick up ants. Spot two.

Archaeotherium used its strong sense of smell to sniff out tasty roots. Spot ten.

23

The Ice ages

During the Ice ages, the climate switched between very warm and extremely cold, with thick snow and ice. Here you can see some of the animals that lived in these different climates.

Columbian mammoths had tusks over 4m (13ft) long. Spot four.

Long-horned bison had poor eyesight. Can you find 12?

Woolly rhinos pushed away the snow with their horns to reach grass. Spot one.

Male cave lions were larger than lions today, but they didn't have manes. Spot one.

Like modern camels, Western camels stored water in their humps. Can you spot two?

Dire wolves used their strong teeth to crush up bones. Find six.

Ground sloths had bony lumps under their skin for protection. Spot one.

Teratornis swooped down to feed on dead animals. Can you find two?

Cave bears went into caves to sleep through the coldest weather. Spot two.

Grey wolves lived and hunted in packs of up to ten animals. Find seven.

Arctic hares had white fur so wolves couldn't see them against the snow. Spot seven.

Herds of ancient bison roamed the plains in search of food. Spot nine.

Reindeer had wide feet to stop them from sinking into the snow. Find ten.

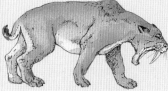

Sabre-toothed cats used their huge fangs to kill other animals. Spot two.

Woolly mammoths had very thick, shaggy fur to keep them warm. Find four.

Western horses died out 10,000 years ago, but no one knows why. Find 12.

Death of the dinosaurs

About 64 million years ago, almost all the dinosaurs died out. No one is certain why. Most scientists believe that an enormous rock from space, measuring up to 10km (6 miles) across, may have hit the Earth.

Clouds of dust

When the rock hit the Earth, it would have caused a huge ball of fire to spread around the world. The rock would have smashed into tiny pieces, surrounding the planet with clouds of dust, rocks and water. The cloud would have blocked out all the Sun's light, making the Earth cold and dark for months.

Animals dying

This would have killed any creatures that needed warmth to survive. Without light, many plants must have died as well, leaving many of the dinosaurs with nothing to eat. The rock may also have caused massive earthquakes and huge tidal waves.

This picture shows what may have happened as the meteorite struck the Earth.

Huge clouds of dust spread out over the Earth, making it hard for animals to breathe.

Dinosaurs were killed or injured by pieces of flying rock.

Dinosaur puzzle

You've already seen all these animals in this part of the book. How much can you remember about them?

You may need to look back to help you with this puzzle. If you get really stuck, you'll find the answers on page 28.

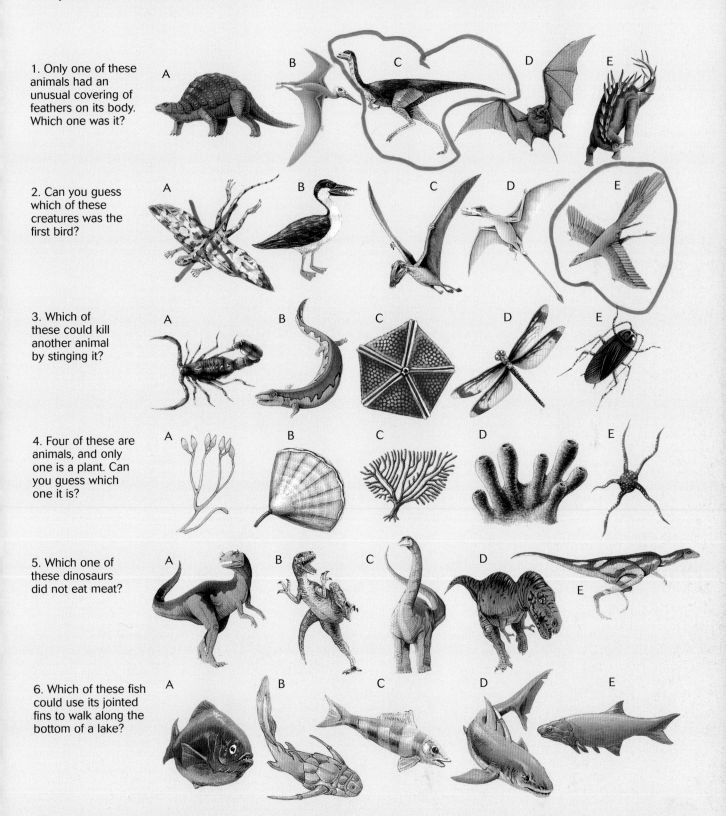

1. Only one of these animals had an unusual covering of feathers on its body. Which one was it?

A B C D E

2. Can you guess which of these creatures was the first bird?

A B C D E

3. Which of these could kill another animal by stinging it?

A B C D E

4. Four of these are animals, and only one is a plant. Can you guess which one it is?

A B C D E

5. Which one of these dinosaurs did not eat meat?

A B C D E

6. Which of these fish could use its jointed fins to walk along the bottom of a lake?

A B C D E

Dinosaur answers

The keys on pages 28 to 31 show you where all the animals and plants you have been asked to spot appear on the pictures in this section of the book. Use the keys if you get stuck trying to find a particular animal or plant.

Answers to the dinosaur puzzle on page 27:

1. C

2. E

3. A

4. A

5. C

6. B

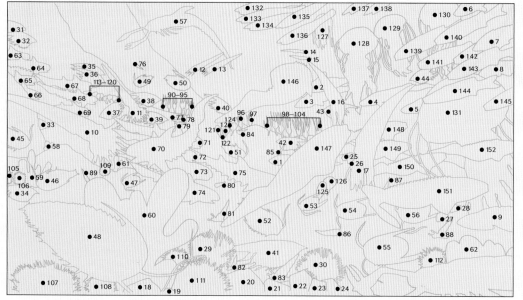

Shallow seas 4–5

Osteostracan fish
1 2 3 4 5 6 7 8 9
Cephalopods 10 11
12 13 14 15 16 17
Starfish 18 19 20 21
22 23 24 25 26
27 28
Graptolites 29 30
Shrimps 31 32 33
34 35 36 37 38
39 40 41 42 43
44
Trilobites 45 46 47
48 49 50 51 52
53 54 55 56
Eurypterid 57
Sponges 58 59 60
61 62
Nostolepis 63 64 65
66 67 68 69 70
71 72 73 74 75
Marine snails 76 77
78 79 80 81 82
83 84 85 86 87
88 89
Sea-lilies 90 91 92
93 94 95 96 97
98 99 100 101
102 103 104

Sea urchins 105
106 107 108 109
110 111 112
Brachiopods 113 114
115 116 117 118
119 120 121 122
123 124 125 126
Jellyfish 127 128 129
130 131
Heterostracan 132
133 134 135 136
137 138
Thelodont 139 140
141 142 143 144
145
Anapsid 146 147 148
149 150 151 152

Living on the land 6–7

Ichthyostegopsis 1 2
Panderichthys 3 4 5
Horsetail plants 6 7
8 9 10 11 12 13 14
15 16 17 18 19
20 21
Water beetles 22 23
24 25 26 27 28
29 30
Woodlice 31 32 33
34 35 36 37 38
39 40
Shrimps 41 42 43
44 45 46 47 48
49 50 51 52 53
54 55
Eusthenopteron 56
57 58
Mimia 59 60 61 62
63 64 65 66 67
68 69 70 71 72
73 74 75 76
Acanthostega 77 78
79 80 81 82 83
Ctenacanthus 84
Groenlandapis 85
86 87 88 89
Ichthyostega 90 91
92 93

Ichthyostega's eggs
94 95 96 97
Aglaophyton 98 99
100 101 102 103
Clubmosses 104
105 106 107 108
109 110 111 112
Bothriolepis 113 114
115 116 117

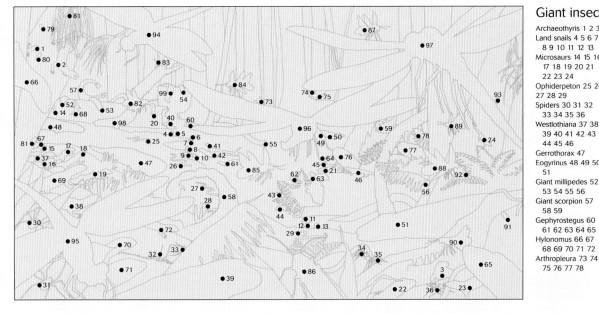

Giant insects 8–9

Archaeothyris 1 2 3
Land snails 4 5 6 7
　8 9 10 11 12 13
Microsaurs 14 15 16
　17 18 19 20 21
　22 23 24
Ophiderpeton 25 26
　27 28 29
Spiders 30 31 32
　33 34 35 36
Westlothiana 37 38
　39 40 41 42 43
　44 45 46
Gerrothorax 47
Eogyrinus 48 49 50
　51
Giant millipedes 52
　53 54 55 56
Giant scorpion 57
　58 59
Gephyrostegus 60
　61 62 63 64 65
Hylonomus 66 67
　68 69 70 71 72
Arthropleura 73 74
　75 76 77 78

Cockroaches 79 80
　81 82 83 84 85
　86 87 88 89 90
　91 92 93
Meganeura 94 95
　96 97
Pholidogaster 98 99

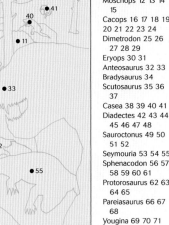

Rocky landscape 10–11

Edaphosaurus 1 2 3
　4 5 6 7 8 9 10 11
Moschops 12 13 14
　15
Cacops 16 17 18 19
　20 21 22 23 24
Dimetrodon 25 26
　27 28 29
Eryops 30 31
Anteosaurus 32 33
Bradysaurus 34
Scutosaurus 35 36
　37
Casea 38 39 40 41
Diadectes 42 43 44
　45 46 47 48
Sauroctonus 49 50
　51 52
Seymouria 53 54 55
　56 57
Sphenacodon 56 57
　58 59 60 61
Protorosaurus 62 63
　64 65
Pareiasaurus 66 67
　68
Youngina 69 70 71

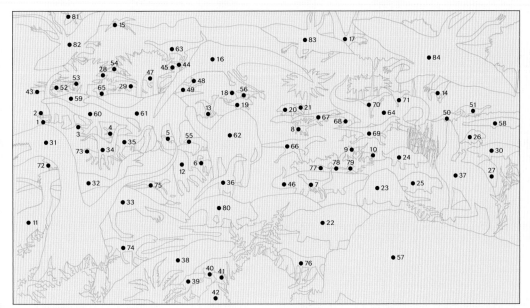

The first dinosaurs 12–13

Saltopus 1 2 3 4 5 6
　7 8 9 10
Syntarsus 11 12 13
　14
Peteinosaurus 15 16
　17
Placerias 18 19 20
　21 22 23 24 25
　26 27
Desmatosuchus 28
　29 30
Coelophysis 31 32
　33 34 35 36 37
Thrinaxodon 38 39
　40 41 42
Stagonolepis 43 44
　45 46
Anchisaurus 47 48
　49 50 51
Ticinosuchus 52 53
　54 55 56
Rutiodon 57 58
Plateosaurus 59 60
　61 62 63 64
Staurikosaurus 65
　66 67 68 69 70
　71

Terrestrisuchus 72
　73 74 75 76 77
　78 79
Cynognathus 80
Kuehneosaurus 81
　82 83 84

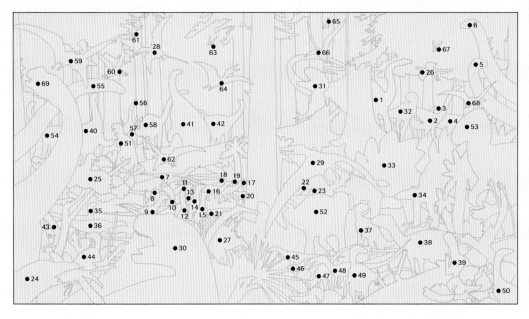

In the forest 14–15

Diplodocus 1 2 3 4 5 6   Brachiosaurus 69

Dryosaurus 7 8 9 10
11 12 13 14 15 16
17 18 19 20 21
22 23

Archaeopteryx 24 25 26

Kentrosaurus 27

Scaphognathus 28 29

Allosaurus 30 31 32

Stegosaurus 33 34

Coelurus 35 36

Ornitholestes 37 38 39

Camarasaurus 40 41 42

Compsognathus 43 44 45 46 47 48 49 50

Ceratosaurus 51

Camptosaurus 52 53

Apatosaurus 54 55 56 57 58

Pterodactylus 59 60 61 62 63 64 65 66 67 68

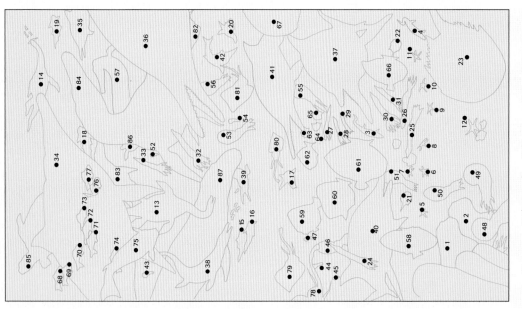

In the ocean 16–17

Pleurosaurus 1 2 3 4   Pleurosternon 85 86

Brittle stars 5 6 7 8 9 10 11 12   Liopleurodon 87

Plesiosaurus 13 14

Sharks 15 16 17 18 19 20

King crabs 21 22 23

Belemnites 24 25 26 27 28 29 30 31 32 33

Ichthyosaurus 34 35 36 37

Geosaurus 38 39

Eurhinosaurus 40 41 42

Ammonites 43 44 45 46 47 48 49 50 51 52 53 54 55 56

Teleosaurus 57

Fish 58 59 60 61 62 63 64 65 66 67 68 69 70 71 72 73 74 75 76 77

Banjo fish 78 79 80 81 82

Rhomaleosaurus 83 84

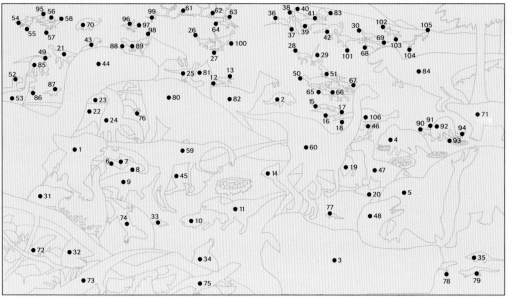

Dusty desert 18–19

Protoceratops 1 2 3 4 5   Psittacosaurus 85 86 87 88 89 90 91 92 93 94

Microsceratops 6 7 8 9 10 11 12 13 14 15 16 17 18 19 20   Oviraptor 95 96 97 98 99 100 101 102 103 104 105 106

Saurornithoides 21 22 23 24 25 26 27 28 29 30

Mammals 31 32 33 34 35

Bractrosaurus 36 37 38 39 40 41 42

Velociraptor 43 44 45 46 47 48

Homalocephale 49 50 51

Avimimus 52 53 54 55 56 57 58

Gallimimus 59 60 61 62 63 64 65 66 67 68 69

Pinacosaurus 70 71

Lizards 72 73 74 75 76 77 78 79

Saurolophus 80 81 82 83

Tarbosaurus 84

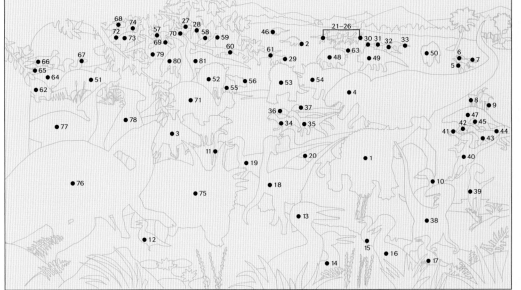

The last dinosaurs 20–21

Euoplocephalus 1 2 3
Tyrannosaurus 4
Stenonychosaurus 5 6 7 8 9 10 11
Ichythornis 12 13 14 15 16 17
Struthiomimus 18 19 20 21 22 23 24 25 26
Stegoceras 27 28 29 30 31 32 33
Dromaeosaurus 34 35 36 37 38 39 40 41 42 43 44 45
Nodosaurus 46 47
Pentaceratops 48 49 50
Triceratops 51 52 53 54 55 56
Pachycephalosaurus 57 58 59 60 61
Panoplosaurus 62 63
Edmontosaurus 64 65 66 67 68 69 70 71

Corythosaurus 72 73 74
Styracosaurus 75
Parasaurolophus 76 77 78 79 80 81

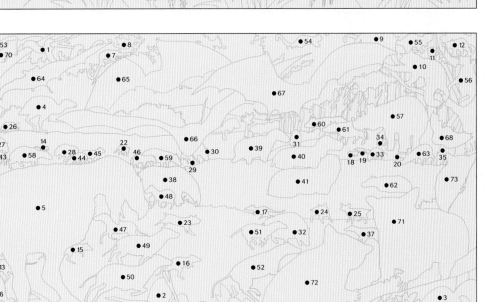

Woodland mammals 22–23

Snake 1 2 3
Diatryma 4 5
Notharctus 6 7 8 9 10 11 12
Leptictidium 13 14 15 16 17 18 19 20
Oxyaena 21 22
Mexonyx 23 24 25
Archaeotherium 26 27 28 29 30 31 32 33 34 35
Eomanis 36 37
Moeritherium 38
Coryphodon 39 40 41
Hyracotherium 42 43 44 45 46 47 48 49 50 51 52
Smilodectes 53 54 55 56
Uintatherium 57
Hyrachus 58 59 60 61 62 63
Bats 64 65 66 67 68
Tetonis 69 70 71 72 73

The Ice ages 24–25

Teratornis 1 2
Cave bears 3 4
Grey wolves 5 6 7 8 9 10 11
Arctic hares 12 13 14 15 16 17 18
Ancient bison 19 20 21 22 23 24 25 26 27
Reindeer 28 29 30 31 32 33 34 35 36 37
Western horses 38 39 40 41 42 43 44 45 46 47 48 49
Woolly mammoths 50 51 52 53
Sabre-toothed cats 54 55
Ground sloth 56
Dire wolves 57 58 59 60 61 62
Camels 63 64
Cave lion 65
Woolly rhino 66

Long-horned bison 67 68 69 70 71 72 73 74 75 76 77 78
Columbian mammoths 79 80 81 82

Part Two
THE
HISTORY
SEARCH

In the town on pages 66 and 67, some poor people lived in a workhouse.

On the American prairies on pages 68 and 69, many people rode in wagons.

Electric stoves were on sale in the department store on pages 70 and 71.

Turn to pages 64 and 65 to see all the people at the French ball in their best clothes.

You'll find this painting of a Dutch family on pages 62 and 63.

The Indian emperor on pages 60 and 61 sat on this beautiful throne.

The palace gardens were lit by paper lanterns at the Chinese party on pages 58 and 59.

Part Two

The Incas on pages 56 and 57 played all kinds of musical instruments.

Jesters lived in medieval castles. See who else lived there on pages 54 and 55.

There was a dancing bear at the village fair on pages 52 and 53.

34

The History Search

Early people painted pictures on their cave walls. See how they lived on pages 36 and 37.

In this part of the book, you can find out about lots of different people and places from history. But this part isn't just about history, it's a puzzle too. The example below shows you how the puzzles work and gives you a few tips to help you solve them.

The farmers on pages 38 and 39 used tools like this sickle.

This strip tells you the date. BC is before Christ and AD is after Christ.

Around the outside of each big picture, there are lots of little pictures.

The writing next to each little picture tells you how many of that thing you can find in the big picture.

This wagon in the distance counts.

People wrote on clay tablets in the Mesopotamian city on pages 40 and 41.

Prairie homes

1870–1880

For many years, the plains, or prairies, of North America were home to Native Americans. Then, settlers from the East took over the land, and built towns and railways. In this town, people are preparing for a holiday.

Find out how the Egyptians built pyramids on pages 42 and 43.

Part of this wall has been taken away, so you can see inside.

This part of a gun counts as one gun.

This cowboy coming out of the big picture counts as a little picture too.

Instead of spotting this printing press, you have to find where it is used.

The Assyrians used siege engines in the battle on pages 44 and 45.

The puzzle is to find all the people, objects and animals in each big picture. Some are easy to spot, but some are tiny, or hidden behind other things.

If the big picture is in two halves (pages 36–37 and 44–45), you will have to look in both halves. You'll find all the answers on pages 72–77.

Find out what the Vikings hung on their walls on pages 50 and 51.

Turn to pages 48 and 49 to find out why Romans took a flask of oil to the bath house.

People at the Greek market on pages 46 and 47 paid with coins like this one.

Early people

The old people told the children exciting stories. Can you find two storytellers?

Fish caught from the river were hung to dry on wooden frames. Spot 20.

Axes were stones on wooden handles. Find two.

People used these digging sticks to dig for roots in the ground. Spot three.

Baskets were woven from rushes. Find nine.

People made tools from flints. Spot four other people chipping away at flints.

People shot animals with bows and arrows. Spot a boy who has shot a bird.

Early people moved around with the seasons, hunting animals and gathering plants to eat. The left-hand page shows some early people in Europe, spending the winter in a cave. The right-hand page shows them in summer.

People painted animal pictures on the cave walls. Spot three deer pictures.

Lamps were made by burning fur soaked in animal fat. Find five.

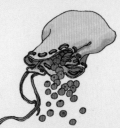

Women gathered berries in leather bags. Find three bags.

Men went hunting for wild animals. Find seven wild deer.

Skins and furs were sewn into coverings and clothes. Find five people sewing.

Babies were wrapped up warmly in animal skins. Can you spot nine?

People scraped skins to clean them. Spot four skins being scraped.

Paint was made from soft rocks and animal fat. Find three people making paint.

People hung skins to dry on wooden racks. Spot five.

Antler

Some tools were made from antlers. Can you find four people carving antlers?

Necklaces were made from shells, stones, bones or teeth. Find 12.

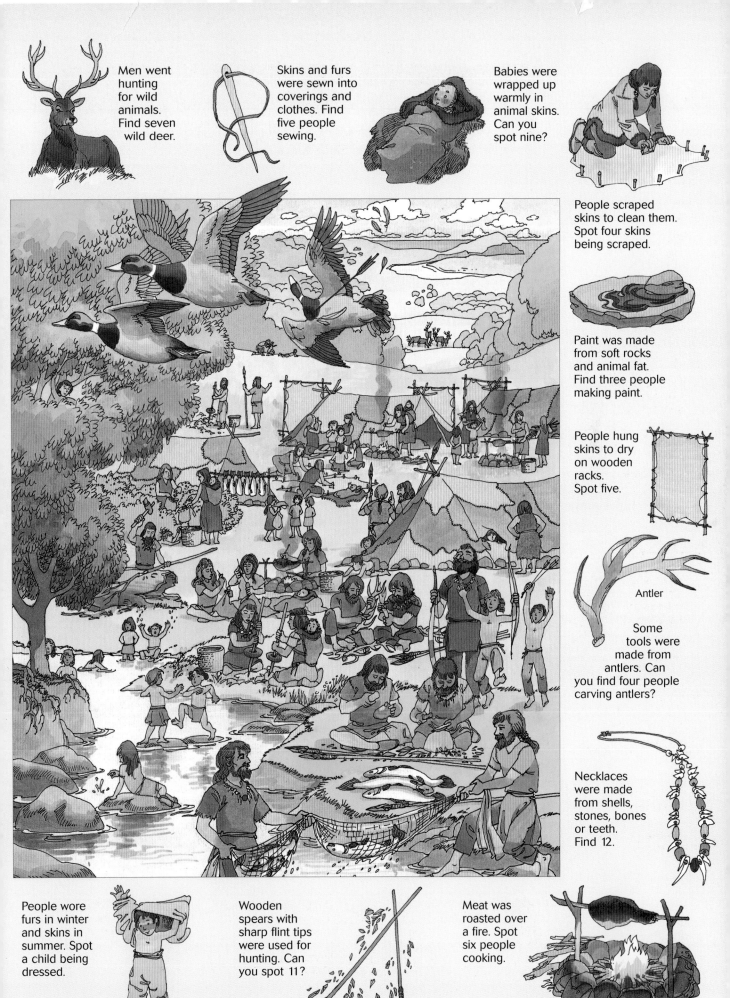

People wore furs in winter and skins in summer. Spot a child being dressed.

Wooden spears with sharp flint tips were used for hunting. Can you spot 11?

Meat was roasted over a fire. Spot six people cooking.

37

Flat loaves of bread were baked on clay ovens. Can you spot eight ovens?

Wooden ladders were used for building. Find three.

Women fetched water from the stream. Find seven women with water pots on their heads.

Spot three cooking pots.

Fish were caught in the stream. Spot four people fishing with nets.

People rolled out pieces of clay to make pots. Find two people making pots.

5000BC

First farmers

At harvest time, crops were cut down with tools called sickles. Spot five sickles.

Farming began when people learned to plant seeds and grow crops. They also tamed animals. These changes meant people could stay in one place instead of moving around. This is a farming village in the Middle East.

Men went hunting for wild animals. Spot two men coming back from a hunting trip.

Women made thread by spinning wool around a spindle. Spot three spindles.

The chief offered gifts to a statue of the village goddess. Find the statue.

Thatched roofs on houses caught fire easily. Find a fire on a roof.

The grain from the crop was put into big baskets. Spot seven baskets.

Find two men mending the mud-brick wall around the village.

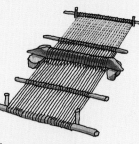
Thread was woven into cloth on a wooden frame called a loom. Spot three.

Sheep were kept for wool, milk and meat. Find 20.

Goats were kept for milk, skins and meat. Find four.

Pigs were kept for meat. Find six pigs and six piglets.

Cattle were kept for milk, skins and meat. Find 16.

Geese were kept for feathers, eggs and meat. Can you spot 11?

Children scared birds away from the crops. Find four children scaring birds.

Children helped look after herds of animals. Find four herders with sticks.

Stones were used to grind grain into flour. Spot four women grinding.

Dogs helped with hunting and herding other animals. Spot eight.

Living in cities

Furniture was made of wood. Spot five chairs.

Most people couldn't read or write, so they hired scribes. Spot one scribe.

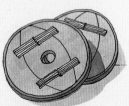

Wheels were made from three pieces of wood joined together. Can you spot ten?

Soldiers wore long cloaks and helmets, and carried spears. Find 16.

Baskets were used for fruit, vegetables and grain. Spot 14.

People used metal tubes as drinking straws. Spot four people using straws.

Early cities had temples, schools and lots of houses. This city is in Mesopotamia. The temple is on a big stepped platform, called a ziggurat. People are going there in a procession, to offer gifts to the city's god.

Buildings had flat roofs. Spot 40 people on rooftops.

Merchants used donkeys to carry packs. Spot four with packs.

Rich boys went to school. Schools were very strict. Spot a schoolboy sneaking in late.

Find four people playing harps like this one.

Spot two pairs of men playing this game.

Dresses were fastened at the shoulder. Find nine women in blue dresses.

People wrote on clay tablets. Spot someone running with a message on a tablet.

Find three metalsmiths who are pouring hot metal into hollow clay shapes.

The king ruled the city. Can you see him in his chariot with the queen?

Potters made clay pots on a wheel. Spot four potter's wheels.

Jars were used to carry wine. Find someone who has broken a jar.

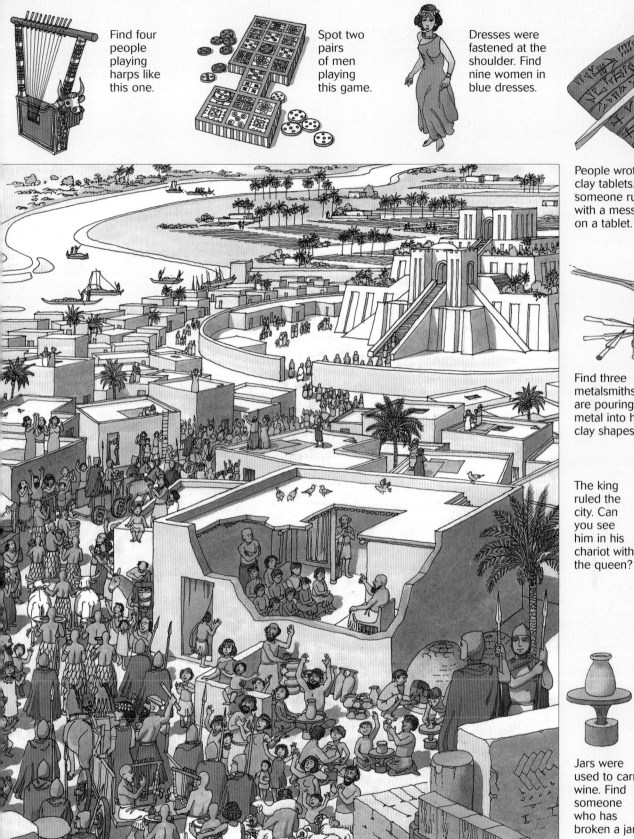

People used seals to sign things. The picture on the seal was rolled into soft clay. Spot one seal.

Stone seal

Rolling the seal

Picture on clay

Can you see a farmer bringing some sheep as a payment to the king?

Pyramids

A ramp of rubble was built to reach the upper levels. Spot someone falling off the ramp.

The king and some other rich people kept pets. Find five dogs.

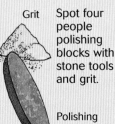

Grit

Spot four people polishing blocks with stone tools and grit.

Polishing tool

The architect planned the building. Can you see him looking at his plans?

Here's the doctor's tool basket. Find the doctor.

The queen had a pet monkey. Spot the monkey being naughty.

Ancient Egyptian kings and queens were buried inside big stone pyramids, which were built while they were still alive. There were no machines, so a pyramid took about 20 years to build. This one is in its early stages.

This is what the finished pyramid looked like. Find two models of finished pyramids.

Mallet

Stonemasons used chisels to chip off rough edges. Can you find six?

Chisel

The king came to check on the work. Can you see him being carried in his chair?

42

Find eight men using wooden poles to lever stone blocks into place.

Teams of men pulled the blocks along on sleds. Find nine sleds.

Carpenters used hammers to mend broken sleds. Spot six hammers.

Measuring instruments were used to check each block was level. Find five.

The queen would have her own pyramid beside the king's. Spot the queen.

Oil was used to help the sleds move smoothly. Spot four jars of oil.

The overseer was in charge of the building work. Can you see him pointing angrily with his stick?

Baskets were used for carrying rubble. Find a man with a hole in his basket.

Birds called hawks looked for food around the building site. Find seven.

Metalsmiths made and mended tools. Spot three saws like this one.

Scribes made lists of how many blocks and tools were being used. Spot six scribes.

43

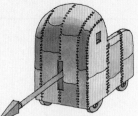

Battering ram

Going into battle

Some soldiers attacked with swords. Find 15 swords.

Siege engines with battering rams inside were used to break through the city walls. Spot five siege engines.

Can you find four horses swimming across the river?

Archers attacked with bows and arrows. Spot 12 bows.

Soldiers wore tunics, leggings and boots. Spot four soldiers putting on their boots.

Spot five soldiers carrying sacks full of stolen goods.

The Assyrian people had a big army of soldiers. The top part of this picture shows the soldiers marching into battle.

The bottom part shows them attacking a city. They stole things and captured people from the places they attacked.

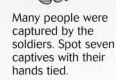

Many people were captured by the soldiers. Spot seven captives with their hands tied.

Some horses wore bright saddle cloths. Spot four yellow cloths.

There was fighting on top of the walls. Spot seven people falling.

The soldiers stole animals. Spot seven sheep being led away.

Even children were captured. Find a mother comforting a child with a drink.

The soldiers carried shields. Spot someone who has dropped his shield.

Inflated skins were used as floats to cross rivers. Spot someone who has let go of his float.

The king rode into battle in his chariot. Can you see him?

Soldiers used ladders made of wood. Can you find eight?

Many soldiers attacked with spears. Spot a broken spear.

Slingers attacked by hurling big stones from leather slings. Can you spot seven others?

Small boats were used to carry things across rivers. Spot four boats.

Scribes made lists of how many people had been killed or captured. Find two scribes.

Soldiers on horseback were called the cavalry. Spot two soldiers on white horses.

At the market

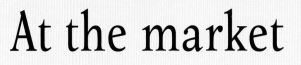

The barber cut people's hair. Find a man who hates his new haircut.

This coin is from Athens. Other cities had their own coins. Spot a man dropping all his money.

Officials checked the weight of things. Find six sets of weighing scales.

People ate olives and used olive oil for cooking and in lamps. Spot someone eating olives.

Can you find four dogs?

Rich people shopped with their slaves. Spot a slave with too much shopping.

This picture shows a busy marketplace in the city of Athens in Greece. A Greek marketplace was called an agora. All the shops were under a covered area called a stoa. Out in the open, there were lots of stalls.

Soldiers had spears and big bronze helmets. Can you see five soldiers?

Cats were rare pets for rich people. Find four cats which have escaped.

Fish was a very popular food. Spot four people who have been to a fish stall.

Find three children playing with hoops.

The wine-seller let some people taste his wine. Spot four people drinking wine.

Can you find three people carrying the sandals they have bought?

Wise men called philosophers met to discuss science and politics. Spot two arguing.

There were often statues of gods or famous people. Find two statues.

Lamps were the only lighting used in houses. Find the lamp stall.

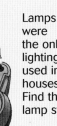
People from outside the city had to change money at the banker's stall. Spot the banker.

Rich people bought slaves. Spot a slave who is trying to escape from his new master.

Some people wore hats when it was sunny. Find five hats.

Pottery was often beautifully painted. Spot five two-handled jars like this.

Actors in plays wore masks like this. Find three actors going to a rehearsal.

The bath house

To relax, people had their bodies massaged by a slave. Spot four people having a massage.

Lots of exercises went on at the baths. Find five people lifting weights.

Spot someone stealing another man's clothes from a changing room locker.

The hot room was called the caldarium. Can you find it?

The Romans made lots of statues. Can you find a statue of the emperor?

People used sticks called strigils to scrape oil and dirt off their bodies. Spot five.

Roman towns had public bath houses, with hot, warm and cold baths. People went to bathe, but also to talk about business, to exercise, or just to gossip. A visit might last hours, and lots of people went every day.

Fighting men called gladiators were very popular. Spot this gladiator with all his fans.

Women went to a separate bath house. Find five women with their towels.

People wore sandals in the hot room, so as not to burn their feet. Spot a man who has forgotten his sandals.

Apartments near the baths were noisy. Find a man who is complaining about the noise.

Instead of soap, people used oil to clean their bodies. Spot 11 oil flasks.

Find eight soldiers with their helmets.

Some floors were covered with mosaics (pictures made from pieces of stone). Spot a mosaic floor.

Attendants worked at the baths. Find an attendant with a pile of towels.

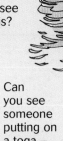

Food, such as pastries and olives, was on sale. Spot two trays of food.

The cold room was called the frigidarium. Can you see where it is?

Can you see someone putting on a toga – a very big piece of material?

People paid to enter the baths. Spot a thief who has run off with someone's purse.

Most large bath houses had a library, with scrolls to read. Find the library.

Scroll

Water was heated by a boiler over a fire. Spot a slave who has fainted from the heat.

Boiler

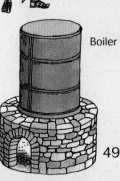

Winter feasts

Cloth was woven on a big loom. Can you see the loom?

Women fastened their tunics with brooches. Find someone doing up her brooch.

Firewood was kept outside. Spot two people gathering wood.

There were spoons and knives, but no forks. Find 12 spoons.

Women wore dresses with tunics on top. Spot someone with a torn tunic.

A poet called a skald played the harp and recited poems. Find the poet.

The Vikings lived in northern Europe. The men were fierce warriors who sailed abroad in their big ships. At home, most Vikings lived in long houses, in small villages. Here, a village chief is giving a feast in his house.

The chief had his own chair. Can you find him?

Wool tapestries hung on the walls. Find a child hiding behind one.

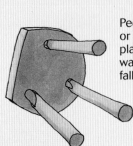

People sat on stools or on wooden platforms along the walls. Spot someone falling off a stool.

When they were not being used, weapons were often hung on the walls. Find five swords.

Beer, wine and mead (a honey drink) were poured from jugs. Spot six.

Acrobats entertained the guests. Find a pair of acrobats.

Food was cooked over an open fire. Spot someone stirring a cauldron full of stew.

The chief had his own servants. Spot a servant with a pile of bowls.

Oil lamps in tall metal holders lit the house. Find five.

People drank from animal horns or wooden cups. Spot 12 drinking horns.

Vegetables and dried fish were hung from the rafters. Spot ten dried fish.

Wine, beer and salted food were stored in wooden barrels. Spot seven.

Men kept hunting dogs. Can you see two fighting?

Clothes and valuable things were kept in chests. Find an open chest.

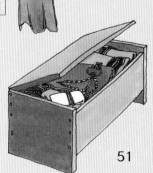

51

Village life

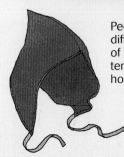

Can you see someone using stepping stones to cross the stream?

In the Middle Ages, most of the people in Europe lived in small villages. A few villagers owned their own land. The rest lived and worked on land owned by a lord. In this English village, the summer fair is being set up.

Merchants came to the fair from nearby towns. Spot a merchant unloading wine from a cart.

Hoe

Houses had vegetable plots. Spot someone using each of these tools.

Rake

Spade

Things for sale at the fair were put on tables. Spot four.

There was lots to see at the fair. Find a dancing bear.

Stocks

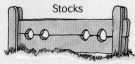

People who did wrong were punished. Spot a man with his legs in the stocks.

The lord lived in a big house or a castle. Can you see him setting off on a hunting trip?

People went to church often. Spot the priest sweeping the church porch.

People wore different kinds of hats. Spot ten pointed hoods.

The blacksmith made and mended metal tools. Can you find him?

Can you see three people chopping firewood outside their houses?

Milk was made into butter in a churn. Spot two churns.

Everyone had their grain ground into flour at the village windmill. Can you see it?

People kept bees for honey. Spot a man being chased by a swarm of bees.

Chickens were kept for meat, feathers and eggs. Spot two people feeding chickens.

Find the miller taking money for grinding some grain.

Can you spot someone going around selling small things from a tray?

Lots of things were bought and sold at the fair. Spot a big pile of cheeses.

Cats were useful for catching rats and mice. Find nine other cats.

Most people had fleas and head lice. Find a woman picking lice from her child's hair.

53

Castle life

In the Middle Ages, kings and lords in Europe built huge stone castles. Armies of fierce soldiers guarded them. The strong, stone walls kept enemies out, but castles were often cold, damp places to live in.

The jester's job was to make people laugh. Spot the jester.

Spot 20 guards on the battlements, looking out for enemies.

The waste from toilets dropped down to the ground below. Can you find two toilets?

Prisoners were kept in the dungeon. Spot a prisoner in chains.

Servants were always busy. Spot a servant with a tray of goblets.

There was enough food stored to last months. Spot the storeroom.

The lord and his wife slept in a big bed with curtains all around it. Find the bed.

This is the lord. Can you see him in his office counting out his money?

Fierce birds called falcons were trained to hunt. Find three.

People didn't wash often. Spot someone in a bathtub.

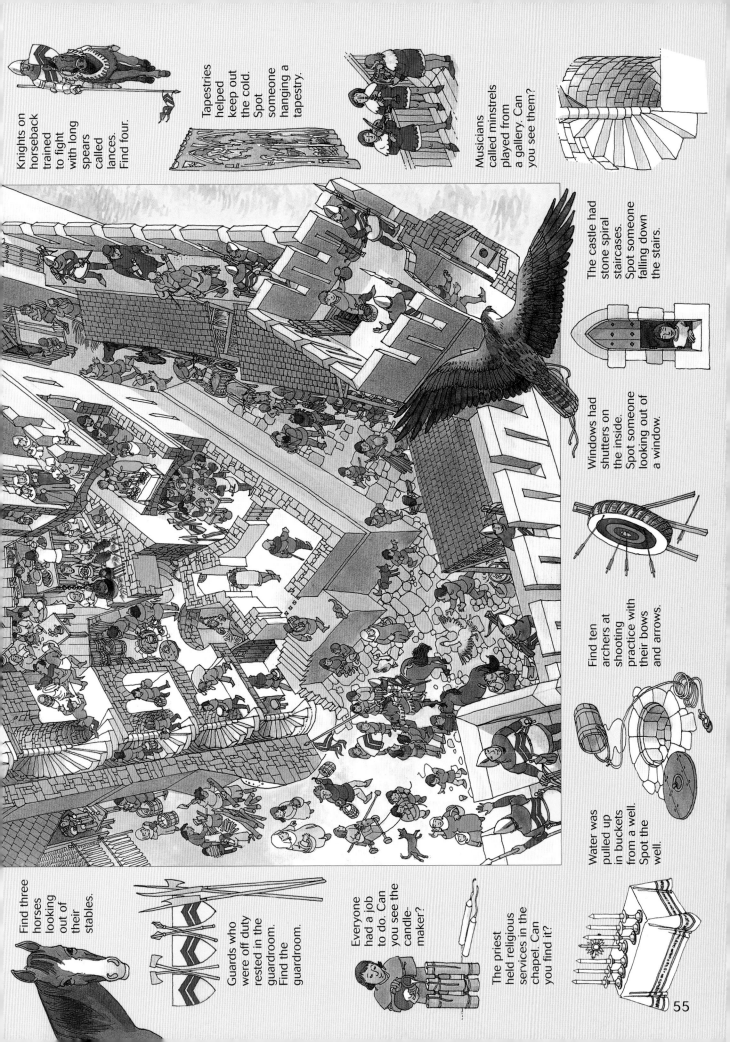

Knights on horseback trained to fight with long spears called lances. Find four.

Tapestries helped keep out the cold. Spot someone hanging a tapestry.

Musicians called minstrels played from a gallery. Can you see them?

The castle had stone spiral staircases. Spot someone falling down the stairs.

Windows had shutters on the inside. Spot someone looking out of a window.

Find ten archers at shooting practice with their bows and arrows.

Water was pulled up in buckets from a well. Spot the well.

Find three horses looking out of their stables.

Guards who were off duty rested in the guardroom. Find the guardroom.

Everyone had a job to do. Can you see the candle-maker?

The priest held religious services in the chapel. Can you find it?

55

Inca homes

Buildings were made from stone blocks which fitted together perfectly. Spot four storehouses.

The soft wool from alpacas was used to make clothes. Find eight.

Bridges were made out of reeds. Spot two.

Women often carried babies on their backs. Find eight babies.

Knotted strings, called quipus, were used to store information. Spot four.

Guinea pigs were not pets, but were kept for meat. Can you find 12?

The Incas lived in the Andes mountains of South America. They built cities and strong stone roads. In this farming village, people are growing crops of corn and potatoes on terraces (steps of land dug into the mountainside).

Llamas were used to carry packs. Find a llama sitting down.

Messengers called chasquis ran quickly to deliver messages. Spot four.

Trumpets called pototos were made from shells. The sound carried far. Find one.

Looms had a strap, which went around the weaver's back. Spot three.

Sandal soles were made of llama skin. Find someone putting on some sandals.

This big mountain bird is a condor. Spot another one.

Spot someone making a drink called chicha by spitting chewed fruit into water.

Potatoes grew well on the high slopes. Find ten sacks of potatoes.

Wooden sticks like this were used for digging. Find ten digging sticks.

Women made flour by grinding corn between stones. Spot a woman grinding.

Cooking pots were all shapes and sizes. Find one like this.

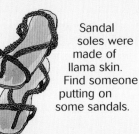

Children scared birds away from the crops by firing stones from slings. Find two slings.

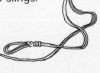

Musical instruments were played on special occasions. Spot each of these.

Panpipes

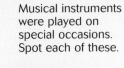

Drum

Flute

The Inca emperor was a strict ruler. Can you see him in his litter, coming to inspect the village?

Litter

A Chinese party

People used fans to keep cool. Spot three fans.

Pottery, clothes and furniture were often decorated with dragon pictures. Find eight.

Silk covers were draped over chairs. Find four chair covers.

People ate rice with almost every meal. Find a half-finished bowl of rice.

Incense burner

People burned incense to make a sweet smell. Spot an incense burner.

Many people kept pet dogs. Find seven.

Chinese emperors and noblemen lived in beautiful palaces with lovely gardens. Most other people in China were poor. In this picture, a rich nobleman is having a firework party. He is sitting on the veranda with his wife.

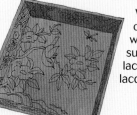

Wood was often covered with a shiny substance called lacquer. Find seven lacquered trays.

Find the palace gardener and his children watching the fireworks.

Gong

Drum

Flute

Musicians entertained the guests. Spot these musical instruments.

Men and women wore silk robes. Find eight red robes.

Fireworks were invented in China. Spot a servant lighting a firework.

Paintings on silk or paper scrolls were hung on walls. Find two.

Officials took notes at important events. Find an official with his boy assistant.

Rich people had statues in their gardens. Find two statues like this.

People poured tea from teapots and drank it from little bowls. Spot four teapots.

Lanterns were made of paper and had candles inside. Spot ten.

People used chopsticks to eat their food. Spot six pairs of chopsticks.

People went to temples but they also had shrines at home for worship. Find one.

Shrine

A type of pottery called porcelain was invented in China. Spot six jars like this one.

Screens were used as doors, or for decoration. They were often painted. Find one.

Indian wedding

Some people rode on elephants, on seats called howdahs. Find five elephants.

The holy man blessed the bride and groom. Can you see him?

Weavers made beautiful things from material. Find these things.

Red and gold wall hanging

Black and white cushion

Blue and green carpet

The palace had lovely gardens. Can you spot a gardener with a spade?

Can you see someone wearing this jewel in his turban?

The Mogul emperors in India were very rich. They lived in grand palaces like this one. Here, everyone is celebrating because the emperor's son is getting married. They are watching the wedding procession.

The emperor's golden throne was decorated with diamonds and rubies. Find it.

People wore gowns called jamas and trousers called piajamas. Spot a man in these clothes.

Yellow jama

Striped piajamas

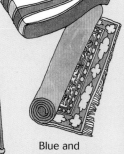

Men wore turbans on their heads. Spot ten dark blue turbans.

Silver bowl

Emerald necklace

Wood and ivory box

Jade wine cup

Mogul craftsmen made lots of beautiful things. Find each of these.

The palace artist painted pictures of important events. Can you find him?

The Moguls had many weapons. Spot a dagger with a horse's head on it.

People smoked pipes called hookahs. Find a man smoking.

Spot the musicians playing these instruments.

Brass trumpet

Drum

Sitar

Tambourine

The bride and groom would not have met before the wedding. Find them.

Groom

Bride

The emperor kept birds at the palace. Find six peacocks.

Most people in India were very poor. Spot this group of beggars outside the palace.

61

Busy ports

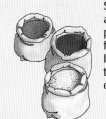

Spices, such as ginger and pepper, came from the East Indies. Spot three sacks of spices.

Sailors used astrolabes on voyages, to measure the height of stars. Can you see one?

In the 1600s, Holland was a very rich country. Big ships, owned by merchants, sailed abroad to buy and sell goods. This is a busy Dutch port. A big ship has just arrived home from a long voyage and is being unloaded.

There were lots of jobs to be done, even in port. Find these workers.

Rope-fitter

Sail mender

Carpenter

Most houses were tall and narrow, with a top part called a gable. Spot a green gable.

Goods were pulled up to storerooms in attics by machines called winches. Find three.

On long voyages, fresh food ran out, so many sailors became ill or died. Spot a sick sailor.

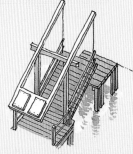

As well as roads, many Dutch towns had canals. Find an open bridge over a canal.

Tulips were rare and expensive. Can you see some?

Artists painted pictures of merchants and their families. Spot an artist.

Ships had guns in case they were attacked by enemies. Find four guns.

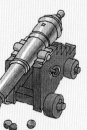
The ship owner paid the crew after each voyage. Find him.

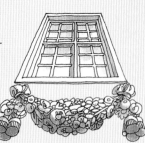

Many houses had stone fruit garlands, called swags, under their windows. Find six swags.

Sailors were often injured on voyages. Spot a sailor who has a wooden leg.

People played musical instruments at home. Find this virginal.

Rich people had servants. Spot the servants who are doing these jobs.

Hanging up laundry

Scrubbing floor tiles

Polishing silver

The telescope was invented in Holland. Spot a scientist using his telescope.

Many goods, such as tea and sugar, came from China, India or Africa. Find these things.

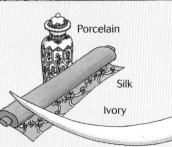
Porcelain

Silk

Ivory

Some rich people ran homes for orphans. Find two ladies collecting a homeless child.

63

At the ball

There were lots of clocks at the palace. Find two.

Men wore wigs made of goat, horse or human hair. Can you see someone whose wig has fallen off?

Both men and women made up their faces. Spot someone checking his face in a pocket mirror.

Shoes often had fine embroidery and buckles. Find these shoes.

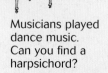

Musicians played dance music. Can you find a harpsichord?

Women curtsied and men bowed to the King. Spot the King.

Jar of smelling salts

The French King Louis XV lived in a fine palace at Versailles, near Paris. He entertained lots of rich people there. In this picture, everyone is at a ball, in a beautiful long room called the Hall of Mirrors.

Women often fainted from the heat. Spot a maid bringing smelling salts to revive her mistress.

The Hall of Mirrors had 17 arched mirrors. Find five of them.

Most people knew the steps for many different dances. Spot a dancer who has fallen over.

The King had hundreds of servants. Can you spot a servant pouring wine?

Dresses had very wide skirts. Find eight pink dresses with this pattern.

Men wore jackets, short trousers called breeches, and silk stockings. Spot a man in these clothes.

Women wore decorations in their hair. Find 11 wearing flowers in their hair.

Women stuck beauty spots on their faces. Find four women with beauty spots.

Hanging glass holders called chandeliers held candles. Can you find four others?

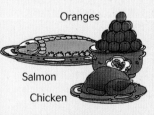

The palace was full of beautiful, expensive furniture. Can you see a couch?

Oranges

Salmon

Chicken

All kinds of tasty food was served at the ball. Spot these dishes.

People drank from crystal glasses. Can you spot someone spilling her wine?

Women carried pretty, painted fans. Find 11 women peeping over their fans.

There were rules about how to behave in front of the King. Spot someone who has misbehaved.

Factory town

Richer people used carriages called hansom cabs as taxis. Find two.

Boats called barges were used to transport heavy goods on canals. Spot three.

People fetched water from pumps in the street. Spot someone pumping water.

Spot the people selling these things from carts or barrows.

Milk

Coal

Fruit and vegetables

Children worked in mines, factories or on the streets. Spot a child selling matches.

Tray of matches

This is a town in England. When big machines for making cloth and other things were invented, many country people moved to towns like this, to work in factories. The streets were noisy, crowded and dirty.

Homeless children and old people were sent to a harsh place called a workhouse. Can you find one?

Steam trains carried passengers and goods all over the country at low cost. Spot a train.

Coal was the main fuel, so lots of people worked down coal mines. Spot six miners with lamps.

Miner's lamp

Sweep's brush

Chimney sweeps climbed up dark, sooty chimneys. Spot three sweeps.

Barber's

Shoemaker's

Tailor's

People bought things from small shops. Find these shops.

Streets were lit by gas lamps. Can you spot ten?

In factories, people worked long hours. Can you spot a tired worker who has fallen asleep?

Newspapers were on sale for people who could read. Spot a paper-seller.

The police tried to stop people from causing trouble or committing crimes. Spot six policemen.

Spot the people doing these jobs on the streets.

Selling pies

Lighting lamps

Selling flowers

Some orphans lived on the streets, stealing money or begging. Spot these beggars.

The filthy streets and houses were full of rats. Spot the rat-catcher doing his rounds.

The barrel organ player entertained people in the street. Can you see him?

Barrel organ

Prairie homes

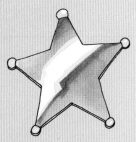

The blacksmith made horseshoes. Can you find him?

The sheriff had to keep law and order. He wore a star-shaped badge. Find him.

People who lived outside town came in to buy things. Spot someone buying this lamp.

There was only one school in town, with one teacher. Find the teacher.

Most people went to church on Sundays. Can you see the church?

There were no phones, but people sent messages by telegraph. Spot six telegraph poles.

For many years, the plains, or prairies, of North America were home to Native Americans. Then, settlers from the East took over the land, and built towns and railways. In this town, people are preparing for a holiday.

BANK

SALOON

RUPERT HEARST

Some people kept on moving West. Spot a family loading their wagon.

The doctor treated people for illnesses or injuries. Can you see him?

Trains carried people, goods and cattle to other towns and cities. Find where the train stops.

Sometimes, robbers tried to steal money from the bank. Spot two.

Most men had guns. Can you find eight guns?

Handgun

Rifle

Men drank and played cards in a bar called a saloon. Spot the barman.

Wagons were used to carry heavy loads. Spot three with covers and three without.

People entertained each other with music. Find these instruments.

Accordion

Piano

Guitar

Some Native Americans lived near the town in areas called reservations. Spot four.

Many people worked on the railways. Spot five men laying new tracks.

Cowboys brought cattle into town. Spot eight other cowboys.

Richer people owned small carriages called buggies. Can you find two?

The local newspaper was printed once a week. Spot the newspaper office.

Printing press

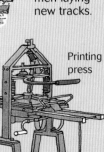

Department stores

When the first department stores opened, people could buy all kinds of things in one building, instead of going to lots of shops.

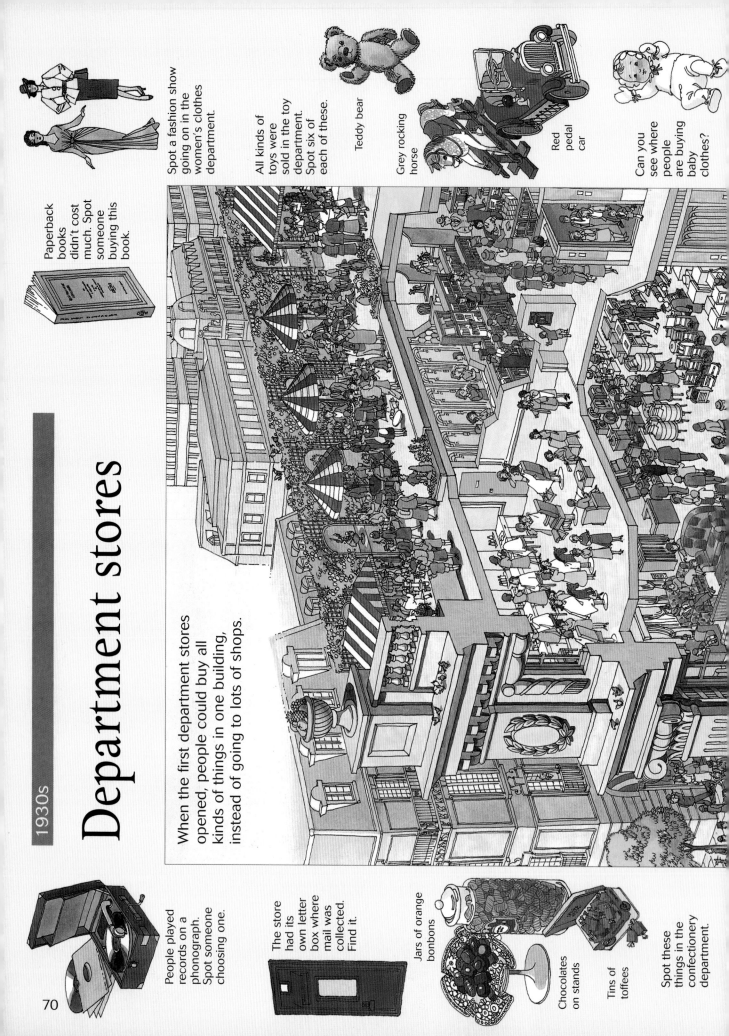

Spot a fashion show going on in the women's clothes department.

All kinds of toys were sold in the toy department. Spot six of each of these.

Teddy bear

Grey rocking horse

Red pedal car

Can you see where people are buying baby clothes?

Paperback books didn't cost much. Spot someone buying this book.

People played records on a phonograph. Spot someone choosing one.

The store had its own letter box where mail was collected. Find it.

Jars of orange bonbons

Chocolates on stands

Tins of toffees

Spot these things in the confectionery department.

70

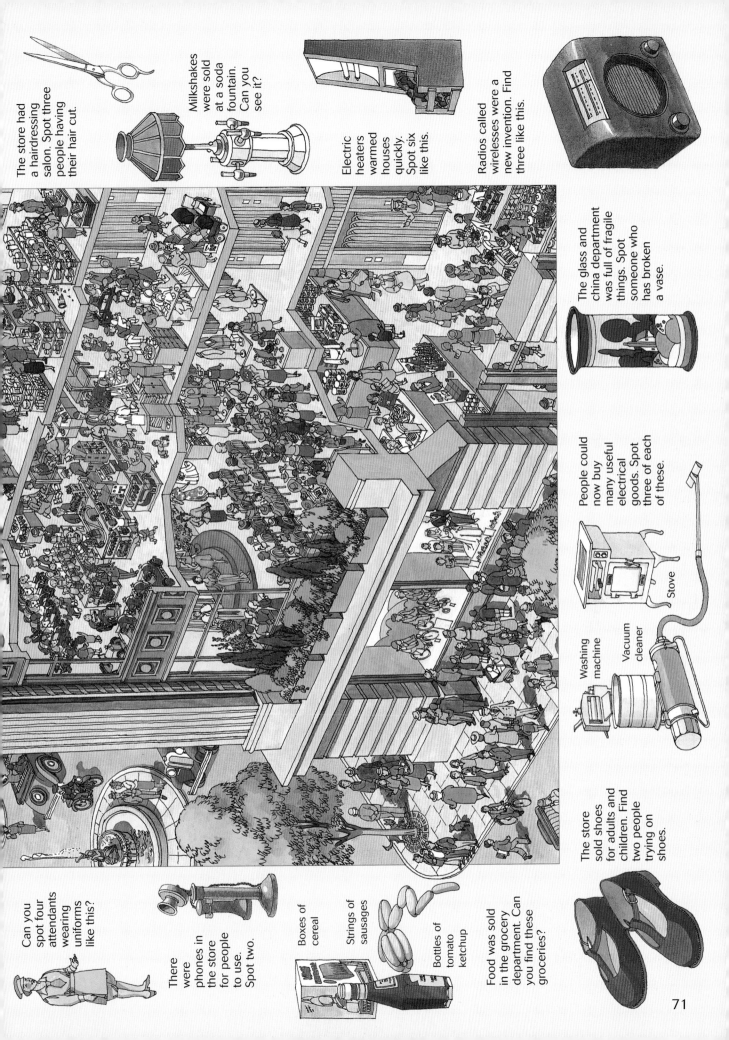

The store had a hairdressing salon. Spot three people having their hair cut.

Milkshakes were sold at a soda fountain. Can you see it?

Electric heaters warmed houses quickly. Spot six like this.

Radios called wirelesses were a new invention. Find three like this.

The glass and china department was full of fragile things. Spot someone who has broken a vase.

People could now buy many useful electrical goods. Spot three of each of these.

Washing machine

Vacuum cleaner

Stove

Can you spot four attendants wearing uniforms like this?

There were phones in the store for people to use. Spot two.

Boxes of cereal

Strings of sausages

Bottles of tomato ketchup

Food was sold in the grocery department. Can you find these groceries?

The store sold shoes for adults and children. Find two people trying on shoes.

71

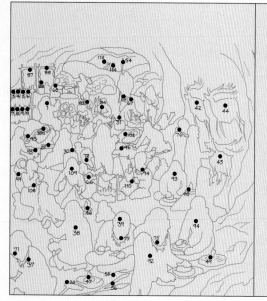
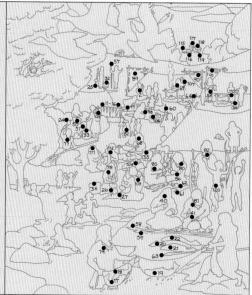

Early people 36–37

Storytellers 1 2
Fish 3 4 5 6 7 8 9
10 11 12 13 14 15
16 17 18 19 20
21 22
Axes 23 24
Digging sticks 25
26 27
Baskets 28 29 30
31 32 33 34
35 36
People chipping
away at flints 37 38
39 40 41
Deer pictures 42 43
44
Lamps 45 46 47 48
49
Leather bags 50 51
52
Child being dressed
53
Spears 54 55 56 57
58 59 60 61 62
63 64
People cooking 65
66 67 68 69 70

Necklaces 71 72 73
74 75 76 77 78
79 80 81 82
People carving
antlers 83 84 85 86
Wooden racks 87
88 89 90 91
People making paint
92 93 94
Skins being scraped
95 96 97 98
Babies 99 100 101
102 103 104
105 106 107
People sewing 108
109 110 111 112
Wild deer 113
114 115 116 117
118 119
Boy who has shot a
bird 120

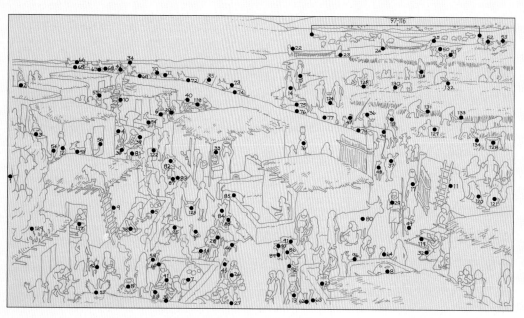

First farmers 38–39

Ovens 1 2 3 4 5
6 7 8
Ladders 9 10 11
Women with water
pots 12 13 14 15 16
17 18
Cooking pots 19
20 21
People fishing 22
23 24 25
People making pots
26 27
Men returning from
hunt 28 29
Spindles 30 31 32
Statue 33
Herders 34 35 36
37
Women grinding 38
39 40 41
Dogs 42 43 44 45
46 47 48 49
Children scaring
birds 50 51 52 53
Geese 54 55 56 57
58 59 60 61 62
63 64

Cattle 65 66 67 68
69 70 71 72 73
74 75 76 77 78
79 80
Pigs 81 82 83 84
85 86
Piglets 87 88 89 90
91 92
Goats 93 94 95 96
Sheep 97 98 99
100 101 102 103
104 105 106 107
108 109 110 111
112 113 114 115
116
Looms 117 118 119
Men mending wall
120 121
Baskets 122 123
124 125 126 127
128
Roof on fire 129
Sickles 130 131 132
133 134

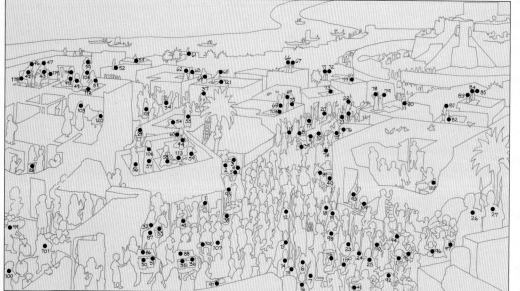

Living in cities 40–41

Scribe 1
Wheels 2 3 4 5 6 7
8 9 10 11
Soldiers 12 13 14 15
16 17 18 19 20
21 22 23 24 25
26 27
Baskets 28 29 30
31 32 33 34 35
36 37 38 39 40
41
People using straws
42 43 44 45
People on roofs 46
47 48 49 50 51
52 53 54 55 56
57 58 59 60 61
62 63 64 65 66
67 68 69 70 71
72 73 74 75 76
77 78 79 80 81
82 83 84 85
Donkeys with packs
86 87 88 89
Late boy 90
Stone seal 91
Farmer with sheep
92

Person who has
broken jar 93
Potter's wheels 94
95 96 97
King 98
Metalsmiths 99 100
101
Messenger 102
Women in blue
dresses 103 104
105 106 107 108
109 110 111
Pairs of men playing
game 112 113
People playing harps
114 115 116 117
Chairs 118 119 120
121 122

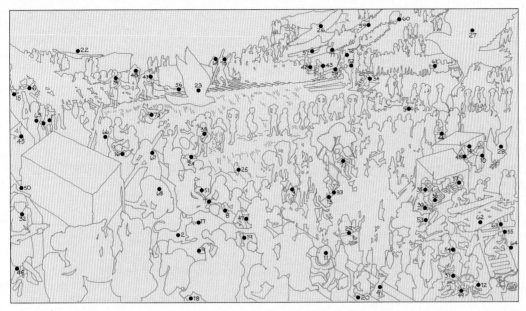

Pyramids 42–43

Dogs 1 2 3 4 5
People polishing 6 7 8 9
Architect 10
Doctor 11
Monkey 12
Pyramid models 13 14
Chisels 15 16 17 18 19 20
King 21
Hawks 22 23 24 25 26 27 28
Saws 29 30 31
Scribes 32 33 34 35 36 37
Man with hole in basket 38
Overseer 39
Oil jars 40 41 42 43
Queen 44
Measuring instruments 45 46 47 48 49
Hammers 50 51 52 53 54 55
Sleds 56 57 58 59 60 61 62 63 64

Men using poles 65 66 67 68 69 70 71 72
Person falling off ramp 73

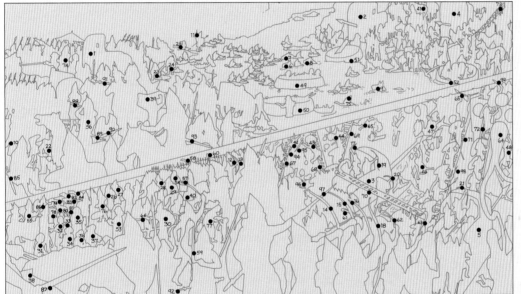

Going into battle 44–45

Siege engines 1 2 3 4 5
Swimming horses 6 7 8 9
Bows 10 11 12 13 14 15 16 17 18 19 20 21
Soldiers putting on boots 22 23 24 25
Soldiers with sacks 26 27 28 29 30
Captives 31 32 33 34 35 36 37
Yellow cloths 38 39 40 41
People falling 42 43 44 45 46 47 48
Boats 49 50 51 52
Scribes 53 54
Soldiers on white horses 55 56
Slings 57 58 59 60 61 62 63 64
Broken spear 65
Ladders 66 67 68 69 70 71 72 73
King 74
Person who has let go of float 75

Person who has dropped shield 76
Mother giving birth to child 77
Sheep 78 79 80 81 82 83 84
Swords 85 86 87 88 89 90 91 92 93 94 95 96 97 98 99

At the market 46–47

Man dropping his money 1
Weighing scales 2 3 4 5 6 7
Person eating olives 8
Dogs 9 10 11 12
Slave carrying too much shopping 13
Soldiers 14 15 16 17 18
Cats 19 20 21 22
People who have been to fish stall 23 24 25 26
Hats 27 28 29 30 31
Two-handled jars 32 33 34 35 36
Actors 37 38 39
Escaping slave 40
Banker 41
Lamp stall 42
Statues 43 44
Philosophers 45 46
People carrying sandals 47 48 49
People drinking wine 50 51 52 53

Children playing with hoops 54 55 56
Man who hates his haircut 57

The bath house 48–49

People having a
massage 1 2 3 4
People lifting weights
  5 6 7 8 9
Person stealing
clothes 10
Caldarium 11
Statue 12
Gladiator 13
Women 14 15 16 17
  18
Man who has
forgotten sandals 19
Thief 20
Library 21
Slave who has
fainted 22
Person putting on
toga 23
Frigidarium 24
Food trays 25 26
Attendant with
towels 27
Mosaic floor 28
Soldiers 29 30 31
  32 33 34 35 36
Oil flasks 37 38 39
  40 41 42 43 44
  45 46 47

Complaining man 48
Strigils 49 50 51 52
  53

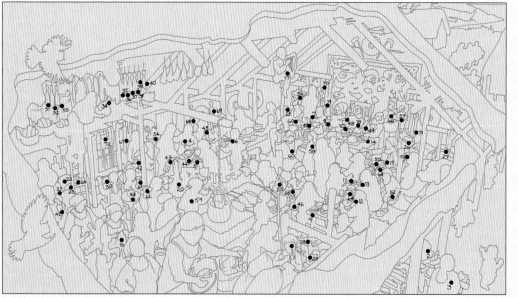

Winter feasts 50–51

Person doing up
brooch 1
People fetching
wood 2 3
Spoons 4 5 6 7 8 9
  10 11 12 13 14 15
Person with torn
tunic 16
Poet 17
Chief 18
Child hiding behind
tapestry 19
Person falling off
stool 20
Barrels 21 22 23 24
  25 26 27
Fighting dogs 28 29
Open chest 30
Dried fish 31 32 33
  34 35 36 37 38
  39 40
Drinking horns 41
  42 43 44 45 46
  47 48 49 50 51
  52
Lamps 53 54 55 56
  57
Servant with pile of
bowls 58

Person stirring
cauldron 59
Pair of acrobats 60
Jugs 61 62 63 64
  65 66
Swords 67 68 69
  70 71
Loom 72

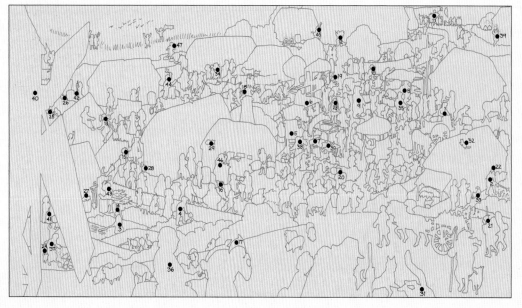

Village life 52–53

Merchant unloading
wine 1
Person using hoe 2
Person using rake 3
Person using spade
  4
Tables 5 6 7 8
Dancing bear 9
Person in stocks 10
Lord 11
Priest 12
Pointed hoods 13 14
  15 16 17 18 19
  20 21 22
Cheeses 23
Cats 24 25 26 27
  28 29 30 31 32
  33
Woman picking lice
from hair 34
Person selling things
from a tray 35
Miller 36
People feeding
chickens 37 38
Man being chased
by bees 39
Windmill 40
Churns 41 42

People chopping
wood 43 44 45
Blacksmith 46
Person using
stepping stones 47

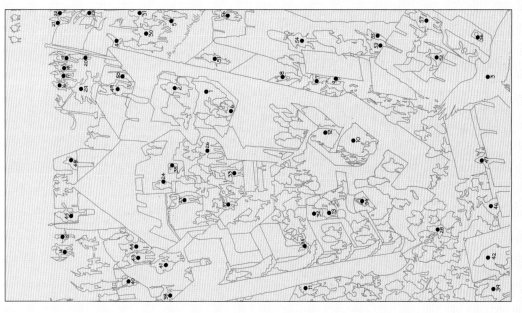

Castle life 54–55

Bed 1
Lord counting
money 2
Falcons 3 4 5
Person in a bathtub
6
Horses looking out
of stables 7 8 9
Guardroom 10
Candlemaker 11
Chapel 12
Well 13
Archers 14 15 16 17
18 19 20 21 22
23
Person looking out of
window 24
Person falling down
stairs 25
Group of minstrels
26
Person hanging a
tapestry 27
Knights on
horseback 28 29
30 31
Storeroom 32
Servant with tray of
goblets 33

Prisoner in chains
34
Toilets 35 36
Jester 37
Guards on
battlements 38 39
40 41 42 43 44
45 46 47 48 49
50 51 52 53 54
55 56 57

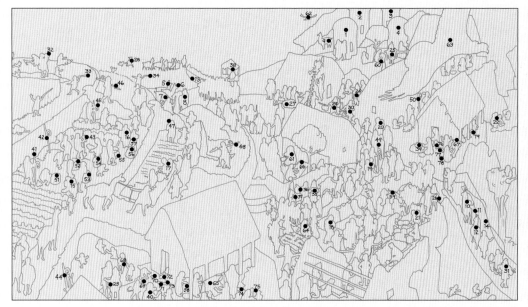

Inca homes 56–57

Storehouses 1 2 3 4
Alpacas 5 6 7 8 9
10 11 12
Bridges 13 14
Babies 15 16 17 18
19 20 21 22
Quipus 23 24 25
26
Llama sitting down
27
Chasquis 28 29 30
31
Pototo 32
Slings 33 34
Panpipes 35
Drum 36
Flute 37
Emperor 38
Cooking pot 39
Woman grinding 40
Digging sticks 41 42
43 44 45 46 47
48 49 50
Sacks of potatoes
51 52 53 54 55
56 57 58 59 60
Person making
chicha drink 61
Condors 62 63

Person putting on
sandals 64
Looms 65 66 67
Guinea pigs 68 69
70 71 72 73 74
75 76 77 78 79

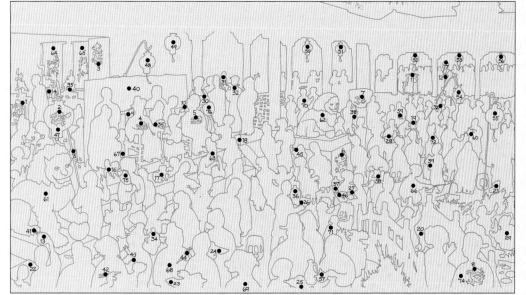

A Chinese party 58–59

Dragon pictures 1 2
3 4 5 6 7 8
Chair covers 9 10 11
12
Half-finished bowl of
rice 13
Incense burner 14
Dogs 15 16 17 18
19 20 21
Lacquered trays 22
23 24 25 26 27
28
Gardener and his
children 29
Drum 30
Gong 31
Flute 32
Shrine 33
Jars 34 35 36 37
38 39
Screen 40
Pairs of chopsticks
41 42 43 44 45
46
Lanterns 47 48 49
50 51 52 53 54
55 56
Teapots 57 58 59
60

Statues 61 62
Official with boy
assistant 63
Paintings 64 65
Servant lighting a
firework 66
Red robes 67 68 69
70 71 72 73 74
Fans 75 76 77

Indian wedding 60–61

Elephants 1 2 3 4 5
Holy man 6
Red and gold wall hanging 7
Black and white cushion 8
Blue and green carpet 9
Gardener with spade 10
Throne 11
Man in yellow jama and striped piajamas 12
Dark blue turbans 13 14 15 16 17 18 19 20 21 22
Bride 23
Groom 24
Peacocks 25 26 27 28 29 30
Group of beggars 31
Musician playing sitar 32
Musician playing tambourine 33
Musician playing drum 34

Musician playing brass trumpet 35
Man smoking 36
Dagger with horse's head 37
Palace artist 38
Jade wine cup 39
Silver bowl 40
Emerald necklace 41
Wood and ivory box 42
Person wearing turban jewel 43

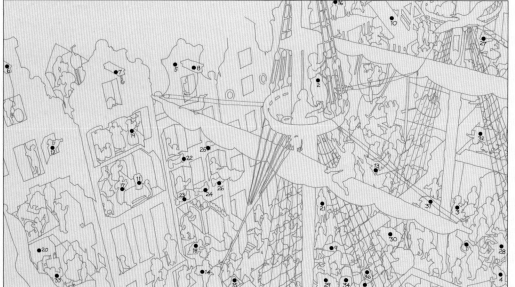

Busy ports 62–63

Astrolabe 1
Rope-fitter 2
Sail mender 3
Carpenter 4
Green gable 5
Winches 6 7 8
Sick sailor 9
Open bridge 10
Tulips 11
Scientist using telescope 12
Ivory 13
Silk 14
Porcelain 15
Ladies collecting orphan 16
Servant polishing silver 17
Servant scrubbing floor tiles 18
Servant hanging up laundry 19
Virginal 20
Sailor with wooden leg 21
Swags 22 23 24 25 26 27
Ship owner 28
Guns 29 30 31 32

Artist 33
Sacks of spices 34 35 36

At the ball 64–65

Person whose wig has fallen off 1
Person checking his face in a pocket mirror 2
Embroidered pink shoes 3
Harpsichord 4
King 5
Maid bringing smelling salts to her mistress 6
Arched mirrors 7 8 9 10 11
Dancer who has fallen over 12
Person spilling wine 13
Women peeping over fans 14 15 16 17 18 19 20 21 22 23 24
Person who has misbehaved 25
Chicken 26
Salmon 27
Oranges 28
Couch 29

Chandeliers 30 31 32 33 34
Women with beauty spots 35 36 37 38
Women wearing flowers in their hair 39 40 41 42 43 44 45 46 47 48 49
Man in blue jacket and green breeches 50
Pink dresses 51 52 53 54 55 56 57 58
Servant pouring wine 59
Clocks 60 61

Factory town 66–67

Hansom cabs 1 2
Barges 3 4 5
Person pumping
water 6
Person selling coal 7
Person selling fruit
and vegetables 8
Person selling milk 9
Workhouse 10
Train 11
Miners 12 13 14 15
    16 17
Beggars 18
Rat-catcher 19
Barrel organ player
    20
Person selling
flowers 21
Person lighting lamps
    22
Person selling pies
    23
Policemen 24 25 26
    27 28 29
Paper-seller 30
Sleeping factory
worker 31

Gas lamps 32 33
    34 35 36 37 38
    39 40 41
Tailor's 42
Barber's 43
Shoemaker's 44
Chimney sweeps 45
    46 47
Child selling matches
    48

Prairie homes 68–69

Sheriff 1
Person buying lamp
    2
Teacher 3
Church 4
Telegraph poles 5 6
    7 8 9 10
Family loading their
wagon 11
Doctor 12
Place where train
stops 13
Cowboys 14 15 16
    17 18 19 20 21
    22
Buggies 23 24
Newspaper office
    25
Men laying new
tracks 26 27 28 29
    30
Native Americans
    31 32 33 34
Guitar 35
Piano 36
Accordion 37

Wagons with covers
    38 39 40
Wagons without
covers 41 42 43
Barman 44
Guns 45 46 47 48
    49 50 51 52
Robbers 53 54
Blacksmith 55

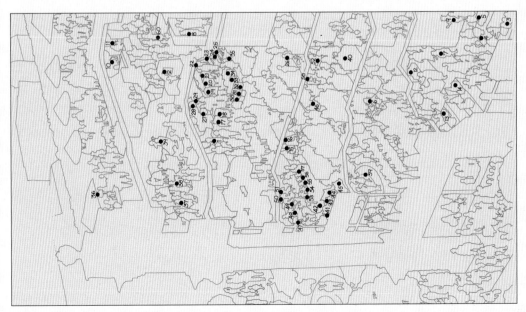

Department stores 70–71

Person choosing
phonograph 1
Letter box 2
Jar of orange
bonbons 3
Chocolates on
stands 4
Tins of toffees 5
Attendants 6 7 8 9
Phones 10 11
Boxes of cereal 12
Strings of sausages
    13
Bottles of tomato
ketchup 14
People trying on
shoes 15 16
Washing machines
    17 18 19
Stoves 20 21 22
Vacuum cleaners 23
    24 25
Person who has
broken a vase 26
Brown square
wirelesses 27 28 29
Pink electric heaters
    30 31 32 33 34
    35

Soda fountain 36
People having their
hair cut 37 38 39
Place where people
are buying baby
clothes 40
Red pedal cars 41
    42 43 44 45 46
Grey rocking horses
    47 48 49 50 51
    52
Teddy bears 53 54
    55 56 57 58
Fashion show 59
Person buying
orange book 60

What are they doing?

You can find each of these people somewhere in the little pictures earlier in this book. To do this puzzle, you'll need to look back and find where they come from.

1. Which of these people is painting a picture?
A B C D E F

2. Which of these children is late for school?
A B C D E F

3. Which of these people is going into battle?
A B C D E F G

4. Which of these women is a queen?
A B C D E F G

5. Which of these people is telling a story?
A B C D E F

6. Which of these pairs of people is in the middle of an argument?
A B C D E

The answers are on page 80.

78

Part Three

THE ANIMAL SEARCH

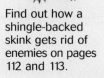

Find out how a shingle-backed skink gets rid of enemies on pages 112 and 113.

Blue whales are the biggest animals of all. You'll find one on pages 114 and 115.

Gardens are busy places. Pages 116 and 117 show you what might live there.

Pigs are just one of the animals you can see on pages 118 and 119.

Bright flame shrimps live on the Barrier Reef, on pages 110 and 111.

Part Three

Tigers hunt in the thick jungles of India. Find out what else lives there on pages 108 and 109.

Snow leopards hunt in high places. Turn to pages 106 and 107 to find out where.

Starfish live on the seashore. Find out what else does on pages 104 and 105.

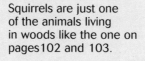

Squirrels are just one of the animals living in woods like the one on pages 102 and 103.

The huge African plains on pages 100 and 101 are home to fast-running cheetahs.

The Animal Search

This creature is a Stegosaurus. Turn to pages 84 and 85 to find out about more kinds of dinosaurs.

You can find out about more than 300 different kinds of animals in this part of the book, but it's not just about animals, it's a big puzzle too. This shows how the puzzles work and gives a few tips to help you solve them.

Skunks make their home in the thick conifer forests on pages 86 and 87.

There are around 100 animals in each big picture. In real life, there would not be as many in the same place at the same time.

Around the outside of each big picture, there are lots of little pictures.

The writing next to each one tells you how many of that animal you can find in the big picture.

American bald eagles glide over swamps on pages 88 and 89.

Mexican red-kneed spiders live in the Sonoran Desert on pages 90 and 91.

This giraffe's horn counts as one giraffe.

A lioness has killed this zebra, but the zebra still counts.

This baby baboon counts as one baboon.

These elephants in the distance count.

Polar bears live in the Arctic. Find out what else lives there on pages 92 and 93.

The puzzly part is finding all the animals. Some are easy to spot, but some are tiny, or hidden against their background. On some pages there's another puzzle too.

If you get stuck, you'll find all the answers on pages 120–125. Every single animal shown in the little pictures that you can find in each big picture counts in your total.

Camels live in the scorching Sahara Desert. Spot more of them on pages 98 and 99.

Sloths find it easy to hide in the thick Amazon Rainforest on pages 96 and 97.

Octopuses are just one of the sea creatures you can find out about on pages 94 and 95.

Tyrannosaurus ate other dinosaurs. It was a ferocious hunter. Find three.

Back in time

Alamosaurus lived on marshy land, munching plants. Find two.

Seventy million years ago, part of North America probably looked like this. Animals called dinosaurs lived here. There are 51 creatures for you to find in this picture. Can you spot them all?

Pteranodon flew on big wings of stretched-out skin. Find two others here.

Parasaurolophus had a curved, bony tube on its head. Can you spot three?

Struthiomimus looked a bit like an ostrich without feathers. Spot seven.

Pachycephalosaurus had a bony lump on its head for head-butting enemies. Can you find three?

Maiasauras laid their eggs in nests. Find one Maiasaura.

84

Deinosuchus' name means "terrible crocodile". Spot two.

Styracosaurus had a bony collar around its neck. Find one.

Ankylosaurus swung its bony tail like a club. Find two.

Quetzalcoatlus was a pterosaur, or "flying lizard". It was as big as a small plane. Spot two.

Stegosaurus had bony plates along its back to protect it from enemies. Find two.

Panoplosaurus was covered with knobs and spikes. Find five.

Anatosaurus had a kind of beak instead of a mouth. Spot three.

Corythosaurus had a hollow, bony plate on its head. Spot four.

Triceratops looked fierce, but it spent its time eating. Find two.

Dromaeosaurus stabbed its enemies with its sharp claws. Spot six.

Conifer forests

Skunks spray smelly liquid at their enemies. Find three.

Black bears are good at climbing trees. Even the cubs can do it. Find four bears.

Forests cover the top of North America and Canada. The trees in them are mainly conifer trees that keep their leaves all year. Not many people live there, but lots of animals do. Can you spot 80 animals in this picture?

Snowshoe hares have furry feet to run in the deep snow in winter. Spot six hares.

Lynxes' beautiful coats blend with the shadows. Can you find three lynxes?

Spruce grouse only eat leaves and buds from spruce trees. Can you find four grouse?

Wolverines are also known as "gluttons". This means greedy people. Find three.

North American martens are fast and fierce hunters. Find three martens.

Chipmunks eat all summer, and sleep all winter. Find eight.

Northern shrikes spend all day feeding their babies. Can you find two?

Long-eared owls have two feathery tufts on their heads. Find four.

Beavers can cut down trees with their sharp teeth. Spot eight beavers.

Crossbills have hooked beaks to dig seeds out of fir cones. Find two.

Moose can wade through water with their long, thin legs. Find six moose.

Fishers attack porcupines. They bite their soft tummies. Spot four fishers.

Brown bears teach their cubs what to eat. Find two and a cub.

Flying squirrels can glide between trees. Spot five squirrels.

Mink slink along looking for voles and insects to eat. Can you find three mink?

Pumas are also called mountain lions or cougars. Spot three.

Ospreys swoop into water to catch fish. Find three.

Porcupines are covered in spikes called quills. Spot three.

Mink slink along looking for voles and insects to eat. Can you find three mink?

Steamy swamps

Green tree frogs have suckers on their feet to climb slimy branches. Find eight frogs.

Otters can even eat fish while swimming on their backs. Spot six.

Snail kites only like eating one kind of snail. Can you find two snail kites?

Zebra butterfly. Spot four.

Fisher spiders eat insects clinging to the bottom of plant stems. Spot one.

Swamps are so wet you can't tell what is land and what is water. Many animals live in these watery worlds.

This picture shows part of a swamp in Florida, in the US, called the Everglades. Can you find 85 animals here?

Gallinules are shy. They hide from enemies in the grass. Find four gallinules.

Gambusia fish eat mosquito eggs. There are plenty in the swamp. Find eight fish.

Bullfrog. Find three.

Bald eagles scoop fish up with their sharp claws. Find two.

Terrapins stick their skinny necks above water to take a look. Find ten.

Little blue herons wait for ages before spearing a fish. Spot two.

Raccoons use their front paws to scoop up fish and frogs from the water. Find six.

Cottonmouth snakes wiggle their bodies to swim along. Spot five.

Orb web spiders spin webs to catch passing insects. Find one.

Snapping turtles are experts at snapping up fish. Can you spot four turtles?

Anhingas dive underwater and stab fish with their beaks. Spot three.

Manatees swim slowly along, munching plants. Spot four.

Pileated woodpeckers keep their babies hidden. Spot three.

Garpike can easily tear up food with their sharp teeth. Spot three.

Dusty deserts

Trapdoor spiders crouch in tunnels and grab insects. Spot two.

Coyotes often howl to each other to keep in touch. Can you find six?

Desert tortoises hide under the sand all day to stay cool. Spot four.

Burrowing owls move into empty burrows rather than dig them. Spot six.

Mexican red-kneed bird-eating spiders are poisonous, but only enough to kill an insect. Find six.

Life is hard in the scorching deserts of North America. One part of them is so hot that it's called Death Valley.

This picture shows part of the Sonoran Desert. If you look closely, you'll spot 95 animals that live in this dusty place.

Loggerhead shrikes push lizards onto cactus spikes. Spot four shrikes.

Black-tailed jackrabbits hop across the hot sand. Spot six jackrabbits.

Gila monsters lick insects' footprints to find them. Find four.

Gambel's quails blend in well with the desert. Can you find two?

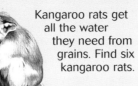

Kangaroo rats get all the water they need from grains. Find six kangaroo rats.

Crafty gila woodpeckers build nests inside cacti. Spot seven.

Rattlesnakes shake their tails to make a scary rattle. Find three rattlesnakes.

Elf owls often move into empty woodpeckers' nests. Find five.

American fringe-toed lizards dig in the sand with their noses and toes. Find eight.

Swallowtail butterfly. Find six.

Roadrunners run in zig-zags, to confuse enemies. Spot three more.

Kit foxes, or swift foxes, run very swiftly across the sand. Find three foxes.

Chuckwallas hide between rocks. Enemies can't see them. Can you spot three?

Peccaries can even eat cacti with their tough teeth. Can you find ten peccaries?

The Arctic

Musk oxen don't mind snow. Their thick coats keep them warm. Can you spot nine?

Thick fur keeps polar bears warm. Spot three and two cubs.

In the Arctic, winter is so cold that the sea freezes. Many animals go to warmer places until spring.

This picture shows the Arctic at the end of a long, cold winter. There are 101 animals here for you to spot.

Humpback whales like this one visit the Arctic. They "sing" as they swim.

Lemmings live in cosy tunnels under the snow all winter. Find 11.

Stoats even squeeze into lemmings' tunnels. Find three stoats.

Baby seals have pale fur which drops out after a few weeks. Spot four.

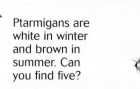

Ptarmigans are white in winter and brown in summer. Can you find five?

Arctic ground squirrel. Find three.

Snowy owls hunt during the long Arctic day. Find three.

92

Raven.
Find
three.

Narwhals have
a horn sticking
out above their
mouths.
Spot two
narwhals.

Arctic foxes
bury animals in
the snow. It's
like a freezer.
Find five.

Wolves often hunt
in a team called a
pack. Spot ten.

Orcas only kill fish
and seals for food.
Find two.

Walruses have
plenty of fat to
keep them warm.
Find 12.

Caribou dig
up plants under
the snow. Spot
11 caribou.

Beluga whale
babies turn
white when they
are two. Find a
mother and baby.

Five kinds of
seals live in
the Arctic.
Find one of
each kind.

Harp seal

Ribbon
seal

Hooded seal

White fur
disguises
Arctic hares
very well. Find
four others.

Bearded
seal

Ringed seal

93

Under the sea

There are more than 20,000 kinds of fish in the world's rivers, lakes and seas. Some fish swim near the surface.

Others live in deep, dark water. This shows 22 kinds of sea creatures in the North Pacific Ocean.

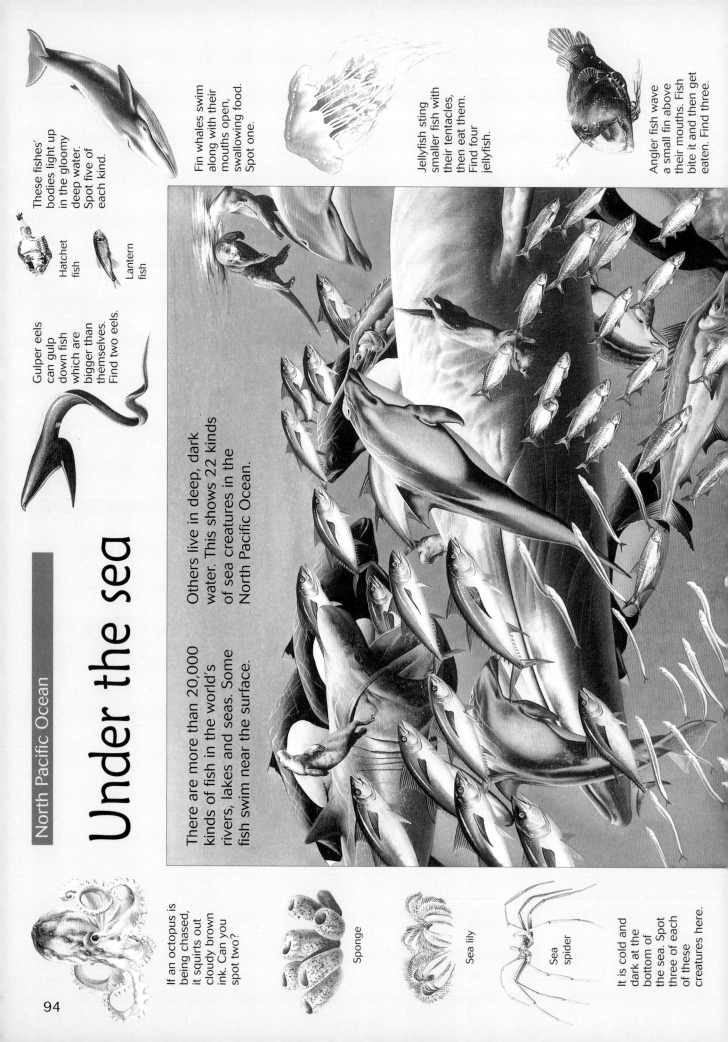

These fishes' bodies light up in the gloomy deep water. Spot five of each kind.

Hatchet fish

Lantern fish

Fin whales swim along with their mouths open, swallowing food. Spot one.

Jellyfish sting smaller fish with their tentacles, then eat them. Find four jellyfish.

Angler fish wave a small fin above their mouths. Fish bite it and then get eaten. Find three.

Gulper eels can gulp down fish which are bigger than themselves. Find two eels.

If an octopus is being chased, it squirts out cloudy brown ink. Can you spot two?

Sponge

Sea lily

Sea spider

It is cold and dark at the bottom of the sea. Spot three of each of these creatures here.

94

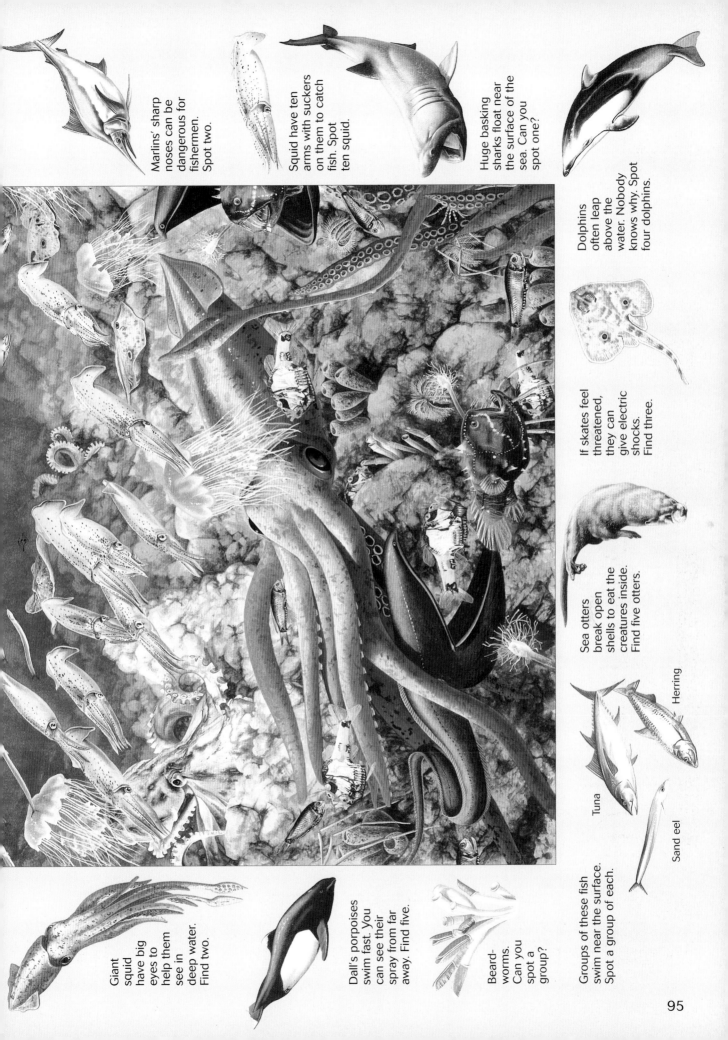

Marlins' sharp noses can be dangerous for fishermen. Spot two.

Squid have ten arms with suckers on them to catch fish. Spot ten squid.

Huge basking sharks float near the surface of the sea. Can you spot one?

Dolphins often leap above the water. Nobody knows why. Spot four dolphins.

If skates feel threatened, they can give electric shocks. Find three.

Sea otters break open shells to eat the creatures inside. Find five otters.

Herring

Tuna

Sand eel

Giant squid have big eyes to help them see in deep water. Find two.

Dall's porpoises swim fast. You can see their spray from far away. Find five.

Beard-worms. Can you spot a group?

Groups of these fish swim near the surface. Spot a group of each.

Tapirs use their long noses to sniff for food among the bushes. Find three.

Emerald tree boas slither through the green trees. They are hard to spot. Find three.

Uakari monkey. Spot six.

Sloths move very slowly. They can spend their whole lives in one tree. Spot three.

Hummingbirds move their wings quickly and make a humming sound. Find three.

Rainforests

Hoatzins are strange birds. They smell awful. Spot two and a baby.

In rainforests, it rains almost every day. Trees and plants grow incredibly fast. This shows part of the Amazon Rainforest in Brazil. More kinds of animals and plants live here than anywhere else. Can you find 71 animals?

Toucans live in pairs. Their huge beaks are made of hollow bone. Spot four.

Black howler monkeys howl to each other to keep in touch. Spot four.

Silky anteaters look for ants. They lick them up with their long tongues. Find two.

Capybaras are good swimmers. They spend most of their time in the water. Spot ten.

Golden lion tamarins have manes of golden hair, like lions. Find three.

Golden cock-of-the-rock. Spot two.

Jaguars climb trees and swim across rivers to catch animals. Find one.

Anacondas can squeeze animals to death. Then they eat them whole. Find three.

Giant armadillos have thick, scaly skin to keep teeth and claws out. Spot two.

Amazon Indians use poison from arrow-poison frogs on the tips of their arrows. Find nine.

Blue and yellow macaw

Coral snakes are poisonous, so animals do not eat them. Spot three.

Spider monkeys are expert tree-climbers. Their tails help them hold on. Find three.

Many kinds of parrots live in the forest. Find one of each kind.

Hyacinth macaw

Golden conure

Scarlet macaw

97

Hot and dry

Camels can last a week without water. Spot eight adults and a baby.

Fennec foxes even hear insects moving with their huge ears. Find four foxes.

Deserts are the hottest, driest places on Earth, but many animals still manage to live in them.

This picture shows part of the Sahara, the biggest desert in the world. Can you find 124 animals?

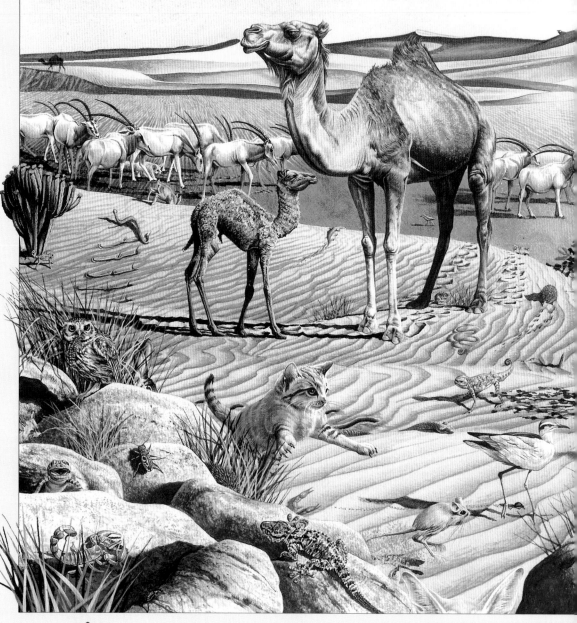

Toad-headed agamid lizard. Spot four.

Desert hedgehogs try to keep out of the sun. Find four hedgehogs.

Mauritanian toad. Spot one.

Desert hares sit in the shade during the heat of the day. Find four hares.

Coursers can run fast to escape from enemies. Find four coursers.

Sahara gecko. Spot one.

Jerboas hop across the sand like mini-kangaroos. Spot five.

Sand vipers bury themselves deep in the sand to stay cool. Find four vipers.

Desert centipede. Spot three.

Find one sandgrouse and her three chicks.

Darkling beetle. Spot three.

Skinks are hard to spot in the desert sand. Find four skinks.

Tiger beetles make a tasty snack for some animals. Spot three.

Little owl. Spot four.

Sand cats hunt smaller animals. Their fur blends in with the sand. Spot four cats.

Desert locusts. Find four.

Sidewinders slither along with an S-shaped wiggle. Find four sidewinders.

Scorpions sting animals with their poisonous tails. Spot three scorpions.

These animals don't mind the heat. They hardly need anything to drink.

Addax. Find five.

Oryx. Spot ten.

Lanner falcon. Find two.

Barbary sheep. Spot 20.

Dorcas gazelle. Spot eight.

Sand rat. Spot three.

Female elephants and babies live together. Male elephants live alone. Find seven.

Cheetahs run faster than any other animal, but they can't do it for long. Spot two.

Gerenuks can stand up on their back legs to reach the tastiest food. Spot two.

When vultures are flying, they can spot a meal a long way away. Spot nine vultures.

African plains

Many of the world's best-known animals live in Africa, on huge, grassy plains. There are 17 kinds of animals here.

If you look closely, you can see what each kind eats. Most eat grass and leaves. Some kill other animals to eat.

Ostriches are birds, but they can't fly. Find three ostriches and their nest.

Big groups of wildebeest wander across the plains looking for food. Find eight.

Rhinos attack enemies by charging at them, horn first. Spot three rhinos.

Baboon babies often ride on their parents' backs. Find eight baboons.

Hippos enjoy soaking in mud. It stops their skin from drying out. Find six.

Giraffes can reach food that no other animal can get to. Find four giraffes.

If a zebra sees an enemy, it barks to warn the others. Spot eight zebras.

Warthogs snuffle along, digging up food with their long tusks. Spot three warthogs.

Wild dogs roam the plains, searching for something to eat. Spot eight.

Thomson's gazelles jump and flash their white bottoms to confuse enemies. Spot ten.

Leopards often drag their food up into a tree to eat it in peace. Find two leopards.

Male lions look fierce, but lionesses do the most hunting. Spot six lions.

Lioness

Lion

Kori bustards are the heaviest flying birds on Earth. Can you find two bustards here?

Hidden homes

Moles tunnel underground. They are almost blind. Spot one.

Spotted fallow deer are hard to see in the shadowy woods. Spot six deer.

Weasels often move into a home that another animal has left. Spot four weasels.

Magpies make messy nests and a lot of noise. Can you spot two magpies here?

Dormice sleep all winter. When they wake up, they start building a home. Spot five.

Woods like this are busy places in the spring. Many animals and birds are making homes for their babies.

There are 18 different kinds of animals in this wood. Can you spot where each kind makes its home?

Wild boar babies are hard to see in the long grass in the woods. Can you spot eight boars?

When a shrew family goes out, each shrew holds on to the one in front. Spot ten.

Jays bury acorns in winter. In spring, they dig them up to eat. Spot four.

 Woodpeckers grip trees with their claws while they eat insects. Find four.

 Several rabbit families live together in one home. Spot nine rabbits.

 Badgers only come out when it is getting dark. Can you spot four badgers?

 Nightjars sit still all day. Their feathers blend well with the woods. Spot two.

 Squirrels build one home for winter and another for summer. Spot four squirrels.

Tawny owls fly silently. They can catch animals without being heard. Spot three.

 If hedgehogs are scared, they roll up into a tough, spiny ball. Spot four hedgehogs.

Both fox parents look after, and teach, their cubs. Can you spot five foxes?

Horseshoe bats only start coming out of their homes as darkness falls. Spot ten.

Stag beetles. Spot two.

Female   Male

103

Most starfish have five arms. If one breaks off, they grow a new one. Spot five.

By the sea

Rotting seaweed is a tasty meal for sandhoppers. Can you spot some sandhoppers?

Redshank use their long, thin beaks to find worms in the mud. Spot three.

Many people visit beaches, but do they know that thousands of animals live under the sand, in pools of seawater or on the cliffs?

The sea covers this beach and goes out again, twice every day. When it is out, the beach looks like this. Can you spot 145 animals here?

Hermit crabs live in empty shells. As they grow, they move into bigger ones. Find four.

Spiny sea urchins push themselves along with their tough spikes. Spot three.

Crabs use their big claws to catch food. They can walk sideways, too. Spot six.

Puffin

Razorbill

Kittiwake

Guillemot

Many birds build their nests on the cliffs. Can you spot ten of each of these kinds?

104

Acorn barnacles grow hard coats around themselves. Can you find some here?

Lobsters are shy, but can give a nasty pinch with their big front claws. Spot two.

Cormorants stand with their wings open, to dry their feathers. Find three.

A snakelocks anemone simply splits in half to make two anemones. Find ten here.

Prawns use their long feelers to search for tiny creatures to eat. Find ten prawns.

On land, beadlet anemones look like blobs. In water, they look like this. Spot five.

Many seashore animals live in hard shells. Spot ten of each of these four kinds.

Mussel   Limpet

Common periwinkle

Dog whelk

Blennies hide in wet places while the sea is out. Spot six.

Oystercatchers knock shellfish off rocks with their sharp beaks. Can you spot six?

Mountains

Bar-headed geese fly over the Himalayas each year. Can you spot ten geese?

Snow leopards, or ounces, hunt at night. They are harder to spot then. Find four.

Himalayan ibexes can clamber up slippery slopes to find food. Spot ten ibexes.

You can probably smell a takin before you see it. They smell oily. Spot two.

Male markhors spend the summer away from the females. Spot three males.

Life is not easy high up in the mountains. It's cold and windy, and the ground is often covered with snow.

The 83 animals here live in the Himalayas, the highest mountains in the world. Can you spot them all?

Himalayan black bears live in forests on the mountain slopes. Find three bears.

Wallcreepers climb down slopes head first. Their claws help them grip. Spot four.

Apollo butterfly. Find three.

If an animal dies, Himalayan griffon vultures swoop down and eat it. Spot six vultures.

Pikas let plants dry in the sun, then store them to eat in winter. Find six pikas.

Lammergeiers fly above the mountains, looking for dead animals to eat. Spot three.

Yaks have a coat of short fur, with long, shaggy hair on top to keep warm. Find five.

Some people think a yeti, or "abominable snowman", made these footprints. Spot some.

Male tahrs have thick fur and a collar of long hair around their heads. Spot three.

While a group of bharals is eating, one keeps a look out for enemies. Spot two.

Alpine choughs push dead insects into cracks in rocks, to eat later. Spot ten choughs.

Marmots sleep in a burrow all winter. They block the door with grass to stay warm. Spot six.

Golden eagles are strong enough to carry off a baby deer. Spot two eagles.

Light and dark

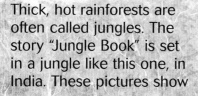

Tigers creep up behind animals. They leap on their backs and kill them. Find one.

Great Indian hornbills like this one use their big beaks to reach any hidden fruit.

Giant flying squirrels glide silently between the trees. Can you spot one?

Gavials catch fish by sweeping their long jaws from side to side. Spot three.

Indian tailor-birds sew nests from leaves and grass. Spot three.

Thick, hot rainforests are often called jungles. The story "Jungle Book" is set in a jungle like this one, in India. These pictures show the jungle by day and at night. Look at both of them and try to spot which of these animals come out during the day and which at night.

Indian elephants often march through the jungle in a line. Find four elephants.

Peacock

Peahen

Male peacocks shake their tails to impress the female peahens. Find one of each.

If muntjac deer are scared, they make barking noises, like dogs. Find two.

Slender lorises even walk on thin twigs, like this. Find one.

Leopards are expert tree-climbers and hunters. Find one leopard.

Dholes are wild dogs. They whistle to each other to stay in touch. Can you find four?

Pangolins curl up into a tight ball. Their scaly skin protects them. Find one.

Lazy sloth bears eat insects, fruit and even flowers. Can you spot a sloth bear?

Leopard cats look like mini-leopards. They are very shy. Can you spot one?

Madras tree shrews live hidden up in the trees, eating insects. Spot one shrew.

Mongooses are brave. They even tease, and then kill, cobras. Spot one mongoose.

Gaurs are a kind of cow. If they are scared, they whistle. Spot two.

The poison from a king cobra's bite can kill a person in half an hour. Spot one.

Bonnet macaques get their name from the tufts of hair on their heads. Spot ten.

Magical world

Bottlenose dolphins often leap over waves, following boats. Spot six dolphins.

If giant clams sense any danger, their huge shells shut tight. Find two giant clams.

Sea squirts. Find six.

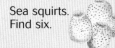

Parrot fish use their hard lips to bite off lumps of coral to eat. Spot two parrot fish.

Sea cucumber. Spot two.

Stone fish lie on the seabed, looking like stones. Can you spot two?

Barracudas are fierce hunters, snapping up other fish. Spot three barracudas.

When tiny sea creatures called corals die, their skeletons are left in the sea. Over thousands of years, millions of these build up to make a reef. The biggest reef in the world is the Great Barrier Reef, near Australia. Can you spot 125 animals and fish here?

Clown fish can hide in poisonous anemones. Find three clown fish somewhere.

Wrasses go into other fishes' mouths and clean their teeth. Spot two.

Snapper

Red emperor

Blue and gold angelfish

Blue damselfish

Spot which fish doesn't belong in each of these five groups.

Goldman's sweetlips

Sea sponge.
Find three.

Dugongs use their big top lip to pull plants from the seabed. Find three.

Sea horse babies grow in a pouch on their father's tummy. Spot six sea horses.

Lion fish. Find two.

Wobbegong sharks often lie still on the seabed, looking like shaggy rugs. Find one.

Bright flame shrimps nibble bugs off fishes' skins. Spot three shrimps.

Tiger cowrie. Spot three.

Manta rays flap through the water with their mouths open, catching food. Find two.

Blue sea star. Find two.

Can you guess how strange-looking hammerhead sharks got their name? Spot one.

There are many different kinds of coral. Can you find a clump of each of these four kinds?

Brain coral

Sea fan

Staghorn coral

Plate coral

Crown of thorns starfish eat coral. They can destroy whole reefs. Find four starfish.

Bright sea slugs slither across the coral. Spot three of each of these kinds of slug.

Naked sea slug

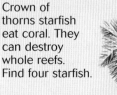

Spanish dancer

Sacoglossan sea slug

111

Out and about

Shingle-backed skinks stick their blue tongues out at enemies. Spot two.

Kangaroos use their big back legs to jump high up into the air. Spot ten.

A lot of Australia is dry land, without many trees. People call it the outback. Not much rain falls, and it's very hot.

Finding enough to eat and drink is tricky. There are 75 animals somewhere in this picture. Can you spot them?

Few animals risk attacking a thorny devil. Its spiky skin is too tough. Spot four.

Marsupial moles are always digging. They rarely come above ground. Find three.

Quolls have long noses for sniffing out food, and sharp teeth to eat it with. Spot two.

Dingos are wild dogs. They live and hunt in a big group. Can you find six dingos?

Kookaburras sound as if they are laughing when they call to each other. Spot four.

Water-holding frogs soak up water like sponges. Spot three.

Mallee fowl lay their eggs in piles of leaves, covered with sand. Find two birds.

Frilled lizards have a fold of skin like a collar around their necks. Spot three.

Bandicoots often dig. Their babies snuggle in a safe pouch under their tummies. Spot two.

Goannas prefer to run away from their enemies than fight them. Spot three.

If echidnas are scared, they bury themselves. Only their spines show then. Spot three.

Hairy-nosed wombats live in underground burrows. Find three wombats.

Budgerigars or parakeets often fly around in a big flock. Find 20 budgerigars here.

Hopping mice usually run, but they can also hop fast on their back legs. Spot two.

Emus are fast runners, but they cannot fly at all. Can you spot three emus?

113

Antarctica

Emperor penguin chicks snuggle between their parents' feet. Spot a chick and five adults.

Sperm whales can stay underwater for an hour before coming up for air. Find one.

Antarctica is the coldest place on Earth. The sea is frozen nearly all year. Icy winds blow across the land.

It's hard to survive here, yet millions of birds and seals do. There are 195 animals and birds for you to find here.

Weddell seals can stay under the freezing water for an hour. Find five.

Rockhopper penguins are good at hopping on snow and rocks. Find 80.

Crabeater seals don't eat crabs. They eat tiny sea animals called krill. Find four.

Blue whales are easily the biggest animals on Earth. Can you spot one here?

Wandering albatrosses glide over the sea on their huge wings. Find one.

Macaroni penguins have feathers called crests on their heads. Spot nine.

Blue-eyed shag. Spot three.

Gentoo penguins lay their eggs in nests made of stones. Spot 21 gentoo penguins.

Ross seals live on the solid ice away from other Antarctic animals. Find four.

Baby minke whales stay with their mothers for about a year. Spot a whale and her baby.

Chinstrap penguins sometimes lay their eggs on snow. Find 12 chinstraps.

Leopard seals catch penguins jumping into the sea. Spot five leopard seals.

Skuas fly over penguins' nests, waiting to kill their chicks. Find four skuas.

Adélie penguins leap from the sea onto the ice. Can you find 13?

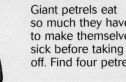

Giant petrels eat so much they have to make themselves sick before taking off. Find four petrels.

King penguins lay one egg. Both parents guard it. Spot ten.

Male elephant seals fight to see who is stronger. Find ten elephant seals.

115

Fox

A closer look

Small white butterfly

Song thrush

Tips:

✿ Birds often come to a garden with a bird-table. They like eating fat, cheese, seeds and nuts.

✿ Lots of animals live in a pond. Others bathe in it, drink from it, or come to catch the animals in it.

✿ A "wild" patch of garden is a great place for insects to hide. Wild flowers might grow there, too.

✿ Berries on plants give birds a tasty meal. Plants that climb walls give them a nesting spot.

✿ Butterflies love bright flowers which smell beautiful. Try planting some in your garden.

✿ Flowerpots make a good home for some animals. Logs are handy for them to shelter under, too.

Animals don't only live in wild places. Lots live in gardens, like this one. There are 31 different kinds here.

Can you find two of each? On this page, there are ideas for things which may make more animals visit your garden.

Garden spider

Robin

Small tortoiseshell butterfly

Vole

Bumblebee

Blackbird

Snail

Earthworm

Wren

Dragonfly

Wood mouse

Woodlouse

Newt

Magpie

Red admiral butterfly

Hedgehog

Centipede

Greenfinch

Earwig

Frog

Slug

Chaffinch

Bullfinch

Peacock butterfly

Toad

Wasp

Mole

Millipede

On the farm

Farmers keep cows for their milk. A cow's baby is called a calf. Can you spot one?

Baby turkeys are called poults. Find three turkey poults.

Farmers train sheepdogs to help control sheep. Find three sheepdog puppies.

Shetland ponies are small but they are hard workers. Find a Shetland foal.

Rats often steal other animals' food. Some farmers poison them. Spot three baby rats.

Farmers keep goats for their milk. Baby goats are called kids. Spot two kids.

Farmers keep animals for their milk, meat, wool or eggs. Wild animals live on farms too. There are 19 kinds of animals in this picture. Each one has some babies hidden somewhere. Can you match the babies to the animals?

Crows eat crops, so farmers make scarecrows to scare them off. Find a baby crow.

Baby geese are called goslings. Feathers called down keep them warm. Find three.

Mice often build their nests in unusual places. Can you find four baby mice?

Cats catch mice and rats. Find three baby cats, or kittens.

Ducks swim on ponds. Find four baby ducks, or ducklings.

Bats sleep all day. Their babies eat at night. Spot two babies.

Shire horses are a kind of large horse. Find a baby shire horse, or shire foal.

Some chickens live inside, others roam outside. Can you spot three chicks?

Pigs roll in muck, but like clean straw to sleep on. Find four baby pigs, or piglets.

Donkeys can carry heavy loads. Can you spot a baby donkey, or foal?

Rabbits live in underground burrows. Can you spot three baby rabbits?

Barn owls hunt at night, swooping on mice and rats. Spot two barn owl chicks.

Baby sheep are called lambs. They are born in the spring. Find two lambs.

119

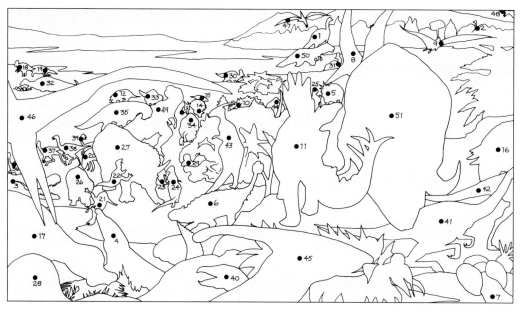

Back in time 84–85

Alamosaurus 1 2
Deinosuchus 3 4
Styracosaurus 5
Ankylosaurus 6 7
Quetzalcoatlus 8 9
Stegosaurus 10 11
Panoplosaurus 12 13
    14 15 16
Anatosaurus 17 18
    19
Dromaeosaurus 20
    21 22 23 24 25
Triceratops 26 27
Corythosaurus 28
    29 30 31
Maiasaura 32
Pachycephalosaurus
    33 34 35
Struthiomimus 36 37
    38 39 40 41 42
Parasaurolophus 43
    44 45
Pteranodon 46 47
    48
Tyrannosaurus 49
    50 51

Conifer forests 86–87

Skunks 1 2 3
Long-eared owls 4 5
    6 7
Beavers 8 9 10 11
    12 13 14 15
Crossbills 16 17
Moose 18 19 20 21
    22 23
Fishers 24 25 26 27
Brown bears 28 29
    30
Flying squirrels 31
    32 33 34 35
Mink 36 37 38
Porcupines 39 40
    41
Ospreys 42 43 44
Pumas 45 46 47
Northern shrikes 48
    49
Chipmunks 50 51
    52 53 54 55 56
    57
Martens 58 59 60
Wolverines 61 62 63
Spruce grouse 64
    65 66 67
Lynxes 68 69 70

Snowshoe hares 71
    72 73 74 75 76
Black bears 77 78
    79 80

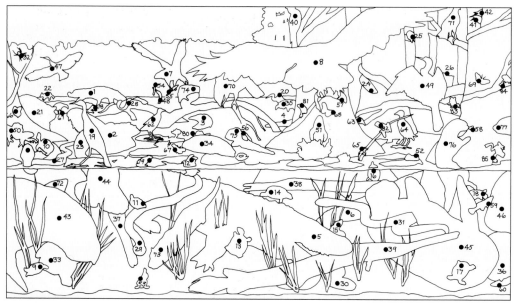

Steamy swamps 88–89

Alligators 1 2 3 4 5
    6
Bald eagles 7 8
Terrapins 9 10 11 12
    13 14 15 16 17 18
Little blue herons
    19 20
Raccoons 21 22 23
    24 25 26
Cottonmouth snakes
    27 28 29 30 31
Orb web spider 32
Snapping turtles 33
    34 35 36
Garpikes 37 38 39
Pileated
woodpeckers 40 41
    42
Manatees 43 44 45
    46
Anhingas 47 48 49
Bullfrogs 50 51 52
Gambusia fish 53
    54 55 56 57 58
    59 60
Gallinules 61 62 63
    64
Fisher spider 65

Zebra butterfly 66
    67 68 69
Snail kites 70 71
Otters 72 73 74 75
    76 77
Green tree frogs 78
    79 80 81 82 83
    84 85

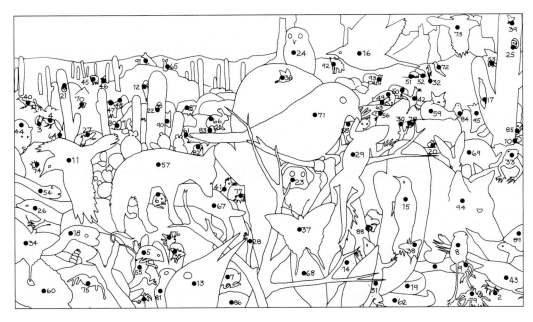

Dusty deserts 90–91

Trapdoor spiders 1 2
Gambel's quails 3 4
Kangaroo rats 5 6 7 8 9 10
Gila woodpeckers 11 12 13 14 15 16 17
Rattlesnakes 18 19 20
Elf owls 21 22 23 24 25
Fringe-toed lizards 26 27 28 29 30 31 32 33
Swallowtail butterflies 34 35 36 37 38 39
Roadrunners 40 41 42 43
Peccaries 44 45 46 47 48 49 50 51 52 53
Chuckwallas 54 55 56
Kit foxes 57 58 59
Gila monsters 60 61 62 63
Jackrabbits 64 65 66 67 68 69

Loggerhead shrikes 70 71 72 73
Mexican red-kneed bird-eating spiders 74 75 76 77 78 79
Burrowing owls 80 81 82 83 84 85
Desert tortoises 86 87 88 89
Coyotes 90 91 92 93 94 95

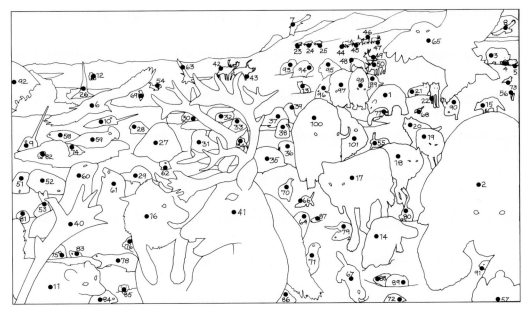

The Arctic 92–93

Polar bears 1 2 3 4 5
Ravens 6 7 8
Narwhals 9 10
Arctic foxes 11 12 13 14 15
Wolves 16 17 18 19 20 21 22 23 24 25
Killer whales 26 27
Walruses 28 29 30 31 32 33 34 35 36 37 38 39
Caribou 40 41 42 43 44 45 46 47 48 49 50
Beluga whales 51 52
Arctic hares 53 54 55 56 57
Ribbon seal 58
Hooded seal 59
Harp seal 60
Ringed seal 61
Bearded seal 62
Snowy owls 63 64 65
Arctic ground squirrels 66 67 68

Ptarmigans 69 70 71 72 73
Baby seals 74 75 76 77
Stoats 78 79 80
Lemmings 81 82 83 84 85 86 87 88 89 90 91
Humpback whale 92
Musk oxen 93 94 95 96 97 98 99 100 101

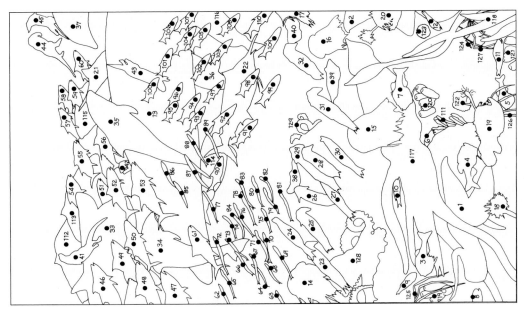

Under the sea 94–95

Gulper eels 1 2
Hatchet fish 3 4 5 6 7
Lantern fish 8 9 10 11 12
Fin whale 13
Jellyfish 14 15 16 17
Angler fish 18 19 20
Marlin 21 22
Squid 23 24 25 26 27 28 29 30 31 32
Basking shark 33
Dolphins 34 35 36 37
Skates 38 39 40
Sea otters 41 42 43 44 45
Tuna 46 47 48 49 50 51 52 53 54 55 56 57 58 59 60 61
Sand eels 62 63 64 65 66 67 68 69 70 71 72 73 74 75 76 77 78 79 80 81 82 83 84 85 86 87 88 89

Herring 90 91 92 93 94 95 96 97 98 99 100 101 102 103 104 105 106 107 108 109 110
Beardworms 111
Dall's porpoises 112 113 114 115 116
Giant squid 117 118
Sponges 119 120 121
Sea lilies 122 123 124
Sea spiders 125 126 127
Octopuses 128 129

Rainforests 96–97

Hoatzins 1 2 3
Capybaras 4 5 6 7 8 9 10 11 12 13
Golden lion tamarins 14 15 16
Cocks-of-the-rock 17 18
Jaguar 19
Anacondas 20 21 22
Giant armadillos 23 24
Arrow-poison frogs 25 26 27 28 29 30 31 32 33
Blue and yellow macaw 34
Scarlet macaw 35
Hyacinth macaw 36
Golden conure 37
Spider monkeys 38 39 40
Coral snakes 41 42 43
Silky anteaters 44 45
Howler monkeys 46 47 48 49

Toucans 50 51 52 53
Hummingbirds 54 55 56
Sloths 57 58 59
Uakari monkeys 60 61 62 63 64 65
Emerald tree boas 66 67 68
Tapirs 69 70 71

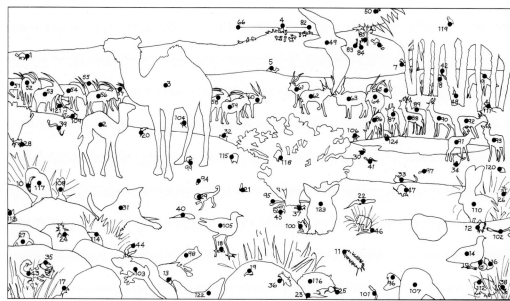

Hot and dry 98–99

Camels 1 2 3 4 5 6 7 8 9
Desert centipedes 10 11 12
Sandgrouse 13 14 15 16
Darkling beetles 17 18 19
Skinks 20 21 22 23
Tiger beetles 24 25 26
Toad-headed lizards 27 28 29 30
Sand cats 31 32 33 34
Desert locusts 35 36 37 38
Sidewinders 39 40 41 42
Scorpions 43 44 45
Sand rats 46 47 48
Lanner falcons 49 50
Oryxes 51 52 53 54 55 56 57 58 59 60
Addaxes 61 62 63 64 65

Barbary sheep 66 67 68 69 70 71 72 73 74 75 76 77 78 79 80 81 82 83 84 85
Dorcas gazelles 86 87 88 89 90 91 92 93
Sand vipers 94 95 96 97
Jerboas 98 99 100 101 102
Sahara gecko 103
Coursers 104 105 106 107
Desert hares 108 109 110 111
Mauritanian toad 112
Desert hedgehogs 113 114 115 116
Little owls 117 118 119 120
Fennec foxes 121 122 123 124

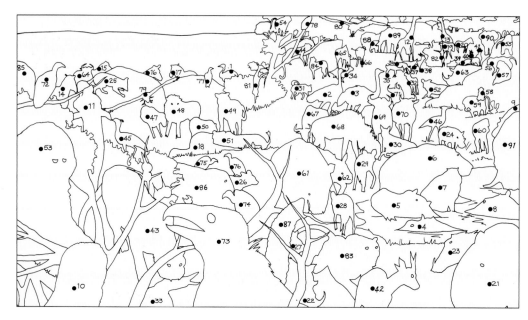

African plains 100–101

Ostriches 1 2 3
Hippos 4 5 6 7 8 9
Giraffes 10 11 12 13
Zebras 14 15 16 17 18 19 20 21
Warthogs 22 23 24
Wild dogs 25 26 27 28 29 30 31 32
Thomson's gazelles 33 34 35 36 37 38 39 40 41 42
Leopards 43 44
Kori bustards 45 46
Lions 47 48 49 50 51 52
Baboons 53 54 55 56 57 58 59 60
Rhinos 61 62 63
Wildebeest 64 65 66 67 68 69 70 71
Vultures 72 73 74 75 76 77 78 79 80
Gerenuks 81 82
Cheetahs 83 84
Elephants 85 86 87 88 89 90 91

Hidden homes 102–103

Mole 1
Woodpeckers 2 3 4 5
Rabbits 6 7 8 9 10 11 12 13 14
Badgers 15 16 17 18
Nightjars 19 20
Squirrels 21 22 23 24
Tawny owls 25 26 27
Hedgehogs 28 29 30 31
Stag beetles 32 33
Horseshoe bats 34 35 36 37 38 39 40 41 42 43
Foxes 44 45 46 47 48
Jays 49 50 51 52
Shrews 53 54 55 56 57 58 59 60 61 62
Wild boars 63 64 65 66 67 68 69 70
Dormice 71 72 73 74 75
Magpies 76 77

Weasels 78 79 80 81
Fallow deer 82 83 84 85 86 87

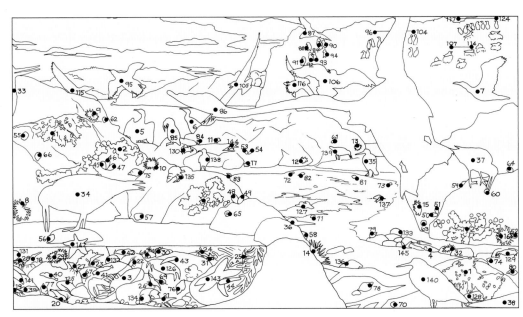

By the sea 104–105

Sandhoppers 1
Barnacles 2
Lobsters 3 4
Cormorants 5 6 7
Snakelocks anemones 8 9 10 11 12 13 14 15 16 17
Prawns 18 19 20 21 22 23 24 25 26 27
Beadlet anemones 28 29 30 31 32
Oystercatchers 33 34 35 36 37 38
Blennies 39 40 41 42 43 44
Mussels 45 46 47 48 49 50 51 52 53 54
Limpets 55 56 57 58 59 60 61 62 63 64
Periwinkles 65 66 67 68 69 70 71 72 73 74
Dog whelks 75 76 77 78 79 80 81 82 83 84

Puffins 85 86 87 88 89 90 91 92 93 94
Guillemots 95 96 97 98 99 100 101 102 103 104
Kittiwakes 105 106 107 108 109 110 111 112 113 114
Razorbills 115 116 117 118 119 120 121 122 123 124
Crabs 125 126 127 128 129 130
Sea urchins 131 132 133
Hermit crabs 134 135 136 137
Redshanks 138 139 140
Starfish 141 142 143 144 145

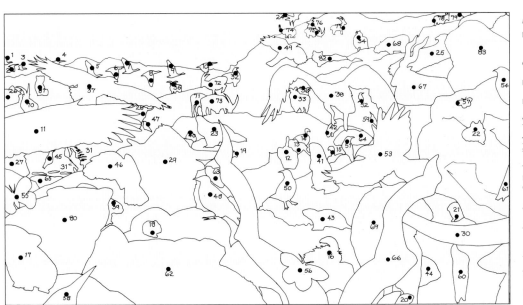

Mountains 106–107

Bar-headed geese 1 2 3 4 5 6 7 8 9 10
Griffon vultures 11 12 13 14 15 16
Pikas 17 18 19 20 21 22
Lammergeiers 23 24 25
Yaks 26 27 28 29 30
Yeti/abominable snowman footprints 31
Tahrs 32 33 34
Bharals 35 36
Golden eagles 37 38
Marmots 39 40 41 42 43 44
Alpine choughs 45 46 47 48 49 50 51 52 53 54
Apollo butterflies 55 56 57
Wallcreepers 58 59 60 61
Black bears 62 63 64

Markhors 65 66 67
Takins 68 69
Ibexes 70 71 72 73 74 75 76 77 78 79
Snow leopards 80 81 82 83

Light and dark 108–109

Tailor-birds 1 2 3
Leopard 4
Dholes 5 6 7 8
Pangolin 9
Sloth bear 10
Leopard cat 11
Madras tree shrew 12
Mongoose 13
Macaques 14 15 16 17 18 19 20 21 22 23
King cobra 24
Gaurs 25 26
Slender loris 27
Muntjac deer 28 29
Peacock/peahen 30 31
Elephants 32 33 34 35
Gavials 36 37 38
Giant flying squirrel 39
Hornbill 40
Tiger 41

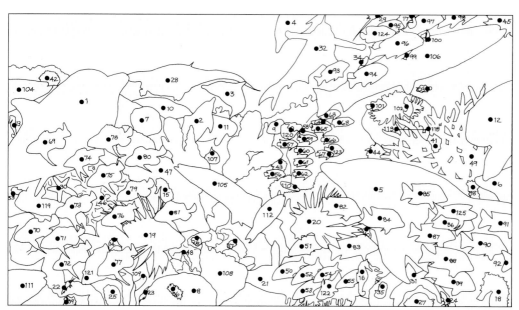

Magical world 110–111

Bottlenose dolphins 1 2 3 4 5 6
Sea sponges 7 8 9
Dugongs 10 11 12
Sea horses 13 14 15 16 17 18
Lion fish 19 20
Wobbegong 21
Flame shrimps 22 23 24
Tiger cowries 25 26 27
Manta rays 28 29
Blue sea stars 30 31
Hammerhead shark 32
Naked sea slugs 33 34 35
Sacoglossan sea slugs 36 37 38
Spanish dancers 39 40 41
Crown of thorns 42 43 44 45
Brain coral 46
Sea fan 47
Plate coral 48
Staghorn coral 49

Snappers 50 51 52 53 54 55
Angelfish 56 57 58 59 60 61 62 63 64 65 66 67 68
Damselfish 69 70 71 72 73 74 75 76 77 78 79 80 81
Red emperors 82 83 84 85 86 87 88 89 90 91 92
Sweetlips 93 94 95 96 97 98
Wrasses 99 100
Clown fish 101 102 103
Barracudas 104 105 106
Stone fish 107 108
Sea cucumber 109 110
Parrot fish 111 112
Sea squirts 113 114 115 116 117 118
Giant clams 119 120
"Odd" fish 121 122 123 124 125

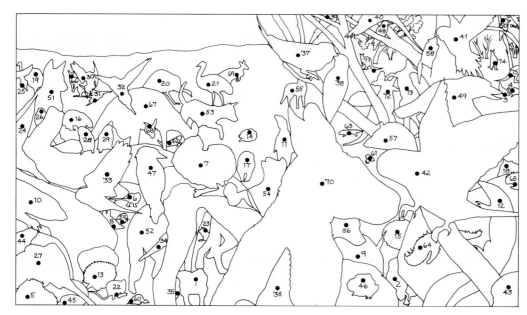

Out and about 112–113

Shingle-backed skinks 1 2
Mallee fowl 3 4
Frilled lizards 5 6 7
Bandicoots 8 9
Goannas 10 11 12
Echidnas 13 14 15
Wombats 16 17 18
Emus 19 20 21
Hopping mice 22 23
Budgerigars/ parakeets 24 25 26 27 28 29 30 31 32 33 34 35 36 37 38 39 40 41 42 43
Water-holding frogs 44 45 46
Kookaburras 47 48 49 50
Dingos 51 52 53 54 55 56
Quolls 57 58
Marsupial moles 59 60 61
Thorny devils 62 63 64 65

Kangaroos 66 67 68 69 70 71 72 73 74 75

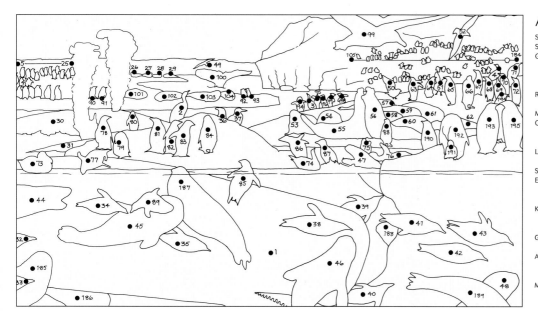

Antarctica 114–115

Sperm whale 1
Shags 2 3 4
Gentoo penguins 5 6 7
  8 9 10 11 12 13 14
  15 16 17 18 19 20
  21 22 23 24 25
Ross seals 26 27 28
  29
Minke whales 30 31
Chinstrap penguins
  32 33 34 35 36 37
  38 39 40 41 42 43
Leopard seals 44 45
  46 47 48
Skuas 49 50 51 52
Elephant seals 53 54
  55 56 57 58 59 60
  61 62
King penguins 63 64
  65 66 67 68 69 70
  71 72
Giant petrels 73 74 75
  76
Adélie penguins 77 78
  79 80 81 82 83 84
  85 86 87 88 89
Macaroni penguins 90
  91 92 93 94 95 96
  97 98

Albatross 99
Blue whale 100
Crabeater seals 101
  102 103 104
Rockhopper penguins
  105 106 107 108
  109 110 111 112 113
  114 115 116 117 118
  119 120 121 122 123
  124 125 126 127 128
  129 130 131 132 133
  134 135 136 137 138
  139 140 141 142 143
  144 145 146 147 148
  149 150 151 152 153
  154 155 156 157 158
  159 160 161 162
  163 164 165 166
  167 168 169 170
  171 172 173 174 175
  176 177 178 179 180
  181 182 183 184
Weddell seals 185 186
  187 188 189
Emperor penguins 190
  191 192 193 194
  195

A closer look 116–117

Foxes 1 2
Small white
  butterflies 3 4
Song thrushes 5 6
Earthworms 7 8
Wrens 9 10
Dragonflies 11 12
Wood mice 13 14
Woodlice 15 16
Newts 17 18
Magpies 19 20
Red admiral
  butterflies 21 22
Hedgehogs 23 24
Centipedes 25 26
Greenfinches 27 28
Earwigs 29 30
Frogs 31 32
Slugs 33 34
Chaffinches 35 36
Millipedes 37 38
Moles 39 40
Wasps 41 42
Toads 43 44
Peacock butterflies
  45 46
Bullfinches 47 48
Snails 49 50
Blackbirds 51 52

Bumblebees 53 54
Voles 55 56
Small tortoiseshell
  butterflies 57 58
Robins 59 60
Garden spiders 61
  62

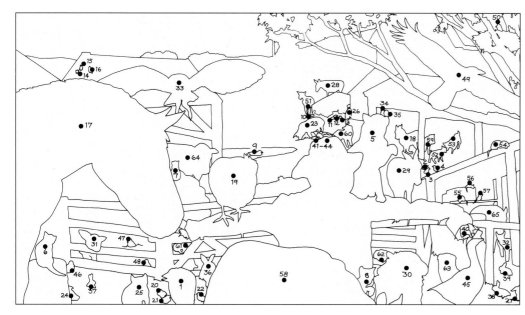

On the farm 118–119

Turkey 1
Turkey poults 2 3 4
Cat 5
Kittens 6 7 8
Duck 9
Ducklings 10 11 12
  13
Baby bats 14 15
Bat 16
Shire horse 17
Shire foal 18
Chicken 19
Chicks 20 21 22
Pig 23
Piglets 24 25 26 27
Donkey 28
Donkey foal 29
Sheep 30
Lambs 31 32
Barn owl 33
Owl chicks 34 35
Rabbit 36
Baby rabbits 37 38
  39
Mouse 40
Baby mice 41 42 43
  44
Goose 45
Goslings 46 47 48

Crow 49
Baby crow 50
Goat 51
Goat kids 52 53
Rat 54
Baby rats 55 56 57
Shetland pony 58
Shetland foal 59
Sheepdog 60
Puppies 61 62 63
Cow 64
Calf 65

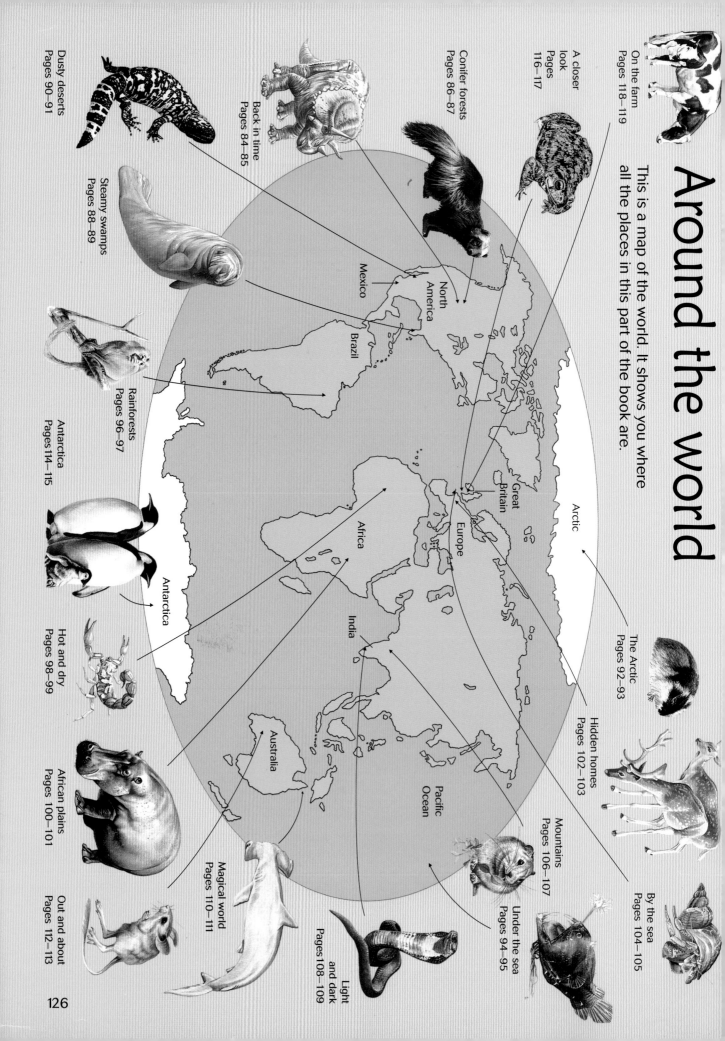

Around the world

This is a map of the world. It shows you where all the places in this part of the book are.

Mexico

North America

Brazil

Great Britain

Europe

Arctic

Africa

Antarctica

India

Australia

Pacific Ocean

Part Four
THE
CASTLE
SEARCH

Part Four

The Castle Search

This part of the book about castles and the people who lived in them. But it's also full of challenging puzzles. You can see below how the puzzles work.

The aim of each puzzle is to spot all the people, animals and objects in the scenes. If you are stuck, you can turn to pages 156 to 159 for help.

The strip at the top of the page tells you where and when the castle in the picture was built.

Around the edge of the big scene are lots of little pictures.

The writing next to each little picture tells you how many of that thing you can find in the big scene.

Some little pictures are shown from a different angle than the ones in the big scene.

Some of the things you are searching for may be partly hidden, but they still count.

The story of castles

A thousand years ago, the world was a very dangerous place. Kings and lords needed somewhere safe to shelter while they fought off attacks. So they started building castles.

The castle provided a home for the lord and his family, his servants and his soldiers. It was also a place of safety for all the people who lived on the lord's land. Whenever an enemy attacked, everyone ran for cover to the castle.

Castles were often built on high ground, so soldiers could keep a lookout for enemies.

Early castles

The first castles were built around the year 900. At first, they were simply strong homes surrounded by banks of earth. But by around 1050 some people were building more complicated structures.

In England and France, kings and lords built 'motte and bailey' castles. These early castles had a tall tower which stood on a mound (or motte), and a walled area known as a bailey. Most people lived in the bailey, but when an enemy attacked everyone sheltered in the tower.

Some early castles had wooden towers, but people soon started building with stone because it was much stronger.

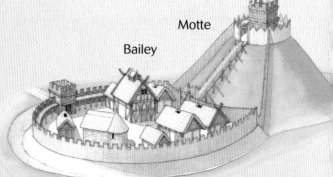

Motte

Bailey

Changing shapes

By the 1300s, armies had developed a terrifying range of weapons. So builders found new ways to make their castles stronger. They built extra walls, with walkways, watchtowers and gatehouses.

Around 1400, soldiers started blasting castle walls with cannons. People no longer felt safe in castles, and the castle as a place of refuge was on its way out.

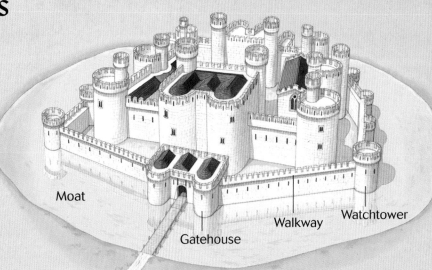

Moat

Gatehouse

Walkway

Watchtower

Heavily defended castles like this were first built by crusader knights fighting in the Middle East.

This romantic castle was built in Germany in the 1860s.

The end of the castle?

By the 1500s, most people had stopped building castles. But many rulers still wanted strong, protected homes. Samurai lords in Japan lived in tall fortresses, while Mogul emperors in India built massive forts from marble and stone.

In the 1800s, some people began to take an interest in castles again. Since then, a few wealthy individuals have built themselves 'mock' castles to live in. These romantic buildings look like medieval castles, but they were never intended for war.

An early castle

After the Normans conquered England in 1066, they forced the Saxon people to build castles.

Many castles had a tower on a mound, or 'motte', and a walled 'bailey', where the soldiers lived.

Norman soldiers were in charge. Find 17 Normans giving orders and watching the Saxons at work.

Carpenters sawed up wood. Spot six carpenters sawing wood.

The castle was protected by a palisade of wooden stakes. Find six workers building the palisade.

A winch was used to lift heavy loads. Can you see the winch?

Castle building could be very dangerous. Spot the falling Saxon.

Sometimes workers took a break. Spot 14 workers having their lunch break.

The castle was surrounded by a ditch. Find 19 Saxons with shovels working on the ditch.

Sometimes workers dropped their tools. Spot two dropped hammers.

Building materials were carried on stretchers and sleds. Find 12 stretchers and three sleds.

Some buildings had thatched roofs made from straw. Spot 17 workers laying or transporting straw.

The castle had three drawbridges. Can you find them?

Lookouts watched out for enemies. Find nine lookouts on the tower and the palisade.

Some people still worked on farms while the castle was built. Spot three farm workers.

Parts of the castle were covered in limewash. Find six builders applying limewash.

135

In the great tower

Many castles had a great tower, built from stone. The tower was the strongest part of the castle, and also the grandest. This was where the lord sometimes stayed and entertained his guests.

Merchants came to visit the lord. Find three merchants.

Tapestries helped to keep out the cold. Spot eight tapestries on the walls.

The tower had steep spiral staircases. Spot the servant falling down the steps.

Religious services were held in the chapel. Can you see three priests?

Looking out for enemies was hungry work. Find the guards having a snack.

Prisoners were captured and held in a bare room. Can you find seven prisoners?

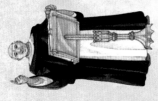

136

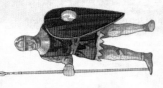

Guards kept a look out for signs of trouble. Find 28 guards on and off duty.

Wooden buckets were used to hold water. Spot 19 buckets of water.

The castle toilet was called the garderobe. Spot a guard on the garderobe.

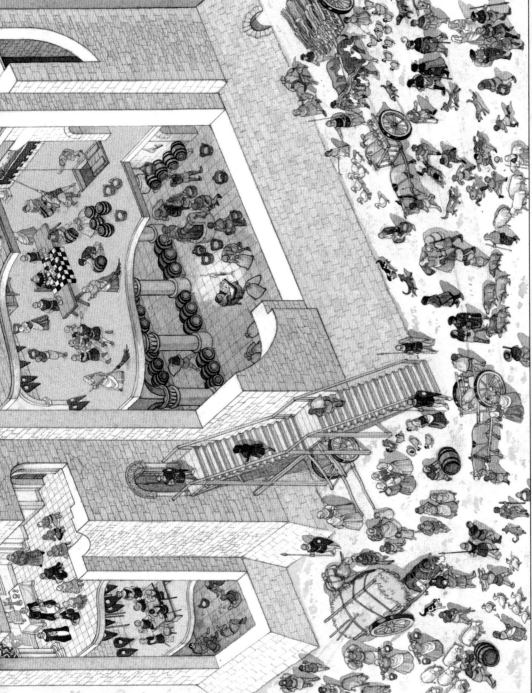

There was enough food stored to last for months. Find 27 sacks of flour and 28 barrels of wine.

The lord held splendid feasts in the Great Hall. Find the lord seated at the high table.

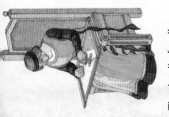

The lord's family stayed in a room called the solar. Find the lady working on her tapestry.

A clerk checked that none of the stores were missing. Can you see the clerk?

The steward was in charge of the castle accounts. Spot the steward counting his money.

In the bailey

The walled area around the great tower was known as the bailey. It was full of people working hard to keep the castle running well. Most of the cooking for the castle was done in the bailey.

Carpenters made furniture and carts. Find a carpenter making a wheel.

Laundry maids spread their washing on bushes. Spot eight tunics drying on the bushes.

Cooks used large cauldrons. Can you see six cauldrons?

Carters arrived with food. Spot 10 turnips that have fallen out of this cart.

Milkmaids carried milk from the castle dairy. Find three milkmaids.

Bakers had large outdoor ovens. Find 16 loaves of bread.

Hunters brought home animals to cook. Spot two deer and eight rabbits.

Blacksmiths made and mended tools and weapons. Find 12 swords being made in the blacksmiths' forge.

Some servants had the job of sharpening knives. Can you see the three knife grinders?

The stables could get quite smelly. Spot five stable boys mucking out the stables.

Farriers made shoes for horses. Find the farrier shoeing a horse.

Children played a kind of football. Spot seven children playing with a ball.

Fletchers made wooden shafts for arrows. Find 13 arrows.

Geese were fattened up for feasts. Spot seven geese.

139

Under siege

During the Middle Ages, castles were often attacked by enemies, and a siege could last for months.

The attackers had some terrifying weapons, but the soldiers under siege fought back fiercely.

Trumpeters gave musical orders to the soldiers. Spot three trumpeters.

Rocks were fired from giant catapults. Find 30 rocks waiting to be fired.

Some soldiers tried to swim across the moat. Spot four swimming men.

Siege towers were wheeled close to the walls. Find 11 men in a siege tower.

Many archers used longbows. Spot 13 longbows.

Some wounded soldiers fell from the battlements. Find three falling defenders.

Dead animals were catapulted into the castle to spread disease. Spot the flying cow.

Knights had shields showing their family's coat of arms. Find 53 shields.

Some archers fired bolts from crossbows. Find six crossbows.

Sometimes an enemy spy sneaked into the castle in disguise. Spot the spy.

Mounted knights fought with violent weapons. Find this morning star.

Daring soldiers climbed scaling ladders. Spot six climbing or falling attackers.

Defenders dropped pots of flaming liquid. Can you spot four pots of fire?

Archers fired through slits in castle walls called arrow loops. Find 20 arrow loops.

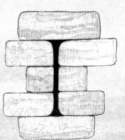

141

At a feast

Sometimes the lord of the castle held a lavish feast in the Great Hall. Important guests sat at the high table, and merchants and knights joined in too. Feasts were very noisy and lasted for hours.

The castle cats and dogs gobbled up the scraps. Spot four cats and four dogs.

Jugglers entertained the guests. Find 11 juggling balls.

The castle servants worked very hard. Can you see six?

Cooks made elaborate dishes from marzipan. Look for the marzipan castle.

The salt container was shaped like a ship. Can you spot it?

Guests drank from gold and silver goblets. Find 31.

The lord's family emblem was displayed in many places. Try to find 10.

Stuffed swan was often served at feasts. Can you see the swan?

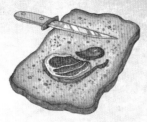

On the lower tables, people used slices of bread for plates. Spot 20.

The hall was lit by candles. Try to find nine.

Roasted boar's head was a popular dish. Can you see it?

Can you find 15 pies dropped by a clumsy page?

Tapestries hung on the walls. Spot five dogs in the tapestries.

Minstrels and entertainers performed during feasts. Find 12.

At a tournament

Tournaments were often held inside a castle's grounds. Daring knights charged at each other in mock battles, called jousts. Lords and ladies sat in decorated stands and many people joined in the fun.

A herald announced the names of the knights. Spot the herald.

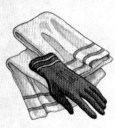

Sometimes a knight wore a lady's token to show his love for her. Can you find two tokens?

A pie seller sold hot pies to the crowd. Can you see nine pies?

Knights jousted with long wooden poles called lances. Try to find 10.

Pages played at being knights. Find the page learning to joust.

The winning knight was given a cup. Can you spot the cup?

Can you see the page who has climbed up to get a better view?

Pickpockets roamed through the crowd. Can you see two?

Even priests came to watch the joust. Find two priests.

Knights wore splendid crests on their helmets. Spot four crests.

Wrestlers fought to see who was the strongest. Try to find four wrestlers.

Visiting knights had their own tents, called pavillions. Spot four pavillions.

Sometimes knights were wounded. Find a wounded knight.

Some people watched the joust from the castle. Spot three ladies on a balcony.

Squires helped their masters at the joust. Find seven more squires.

145

A family home

The lord of the castle and his family didn't live in their castle all the time, but they often stayed there. Here you can see the family in their living room, or 'solar', and in the castle grounds.

The lady of the castle planned feasts with the cook. Find the cook.

Puppets were popular toys. Try to spot seven.

Boys from noble families came to be squires at the castle. Find two squires training to be knights.

Babies had silver rattles. Spot the rattle.

Girls did fine needlework. Spot three pieces of needlework.

The family owned precious handmade books, called manuscripts. Find five.

The lord and his friends went out hunting. Spot six hunting horns.

The older children played chess. Find the chess piece their little sister has taken.

Children played with spinning tops. Try to spot four.

The castle was full of dogs. Find 14 dogs inside and out.

Many people had meetings with the lord. Spot the steward and the constable.

Herbs were grown to make medicines. Spot the lord's mother in her herb garden.

The ladies used falcons to hunt for small birds. Spot six falcons.

Some children rode hobby horses. Can you find six?

147

A crusader castle

Crusaders were Christian knights from Europe who fought to win land around Jerusalem.

This scene shows a king and his followers visiting a castle built by crusader knights.

This castle was run by crusader knights called Hospitallers. Can you spot 33 Hospitaller knights?

Wild animals lurked in the hills. Can you spot six wolves and a lion?

Find a lady who has fainted from heat.

The castle baker ground his flour in a windmill. Spot the windmill.

Can you see the king who has come to stay in the castle?

The crusaders kept pigeons to eat. Find 29 pigeons.

Armed knights accompanied the king. Find nine mounted knights.

Some knights were attacked and wounded on the way. Spot the wounded knight.

Squires walked beside their masters. Can you see six squires?

Mules carried sacks of food supplies. Spot five mules.

Minstrels played to the knights and ladies. Find the minstrel.

The chief guard of the castle was called the castellan. Can you spot him?

Can you spot the bishop giving thanks for a safe journey?

An aqueduct carried water to the castle. Can you see the aqueduct?

A samurai fortress

Japanese war lords lived in well-defended fortresses with their fierce samurai warriors.

In peacetime, the samurai trained for battle and the fortresses were full of life.

The lord of the fortress was called the daimyo. Can you spot him?

Nursemaids cared for the lord's children. Find three nursemaids.

Samurai warriors marched around the courtyard. Spot ten small flags on the backs of the samurai.

Laundry maids washed huge loads of clothes. Find three laundry baskets.

Young samurai learned how to fight. Find eight samurai fighting with wooden swords.

Some Buddhist priests lived in the fortress. Can you see three priests?

Merchants bought silk to show the ladies. Find three merchants bringing silk.

The lord's children loved to fly kites. Can you see five kites?

Local farmers brought food to the fortress. Find four farmers with baskets of food.

Leatherworkers made saddles for the warriors. Spot seven saddles.

Sword-makers sharpened swords on stones. Find four sword-makers.

Tall banners were fixed to the fortress walls and carried by flag-bearers. Spot nine banners.

Samurai wore breastplates made from metal strips. Spot two metalworkers making some breastplates.

Poets and musicians entertained the ladies. Find a poet and two musicians.

A Mogul fort

The Mogul emperors of India built vast, walled forts that contained beautiful palaces, gardens and mosques. This scene shows a Mogul emperor welcoming a procession of guests to his fort.

The emperor sat on a golden throne. Spot the emperor.

There were far more men than ladies at the court. Find 19 ladies in this scene.

Some palace guards were armed with muskets. Can you see four muskets?

Musicians played many different instruments. Spot four drums, nine curved and straight horns, and two pairs of cymbals.

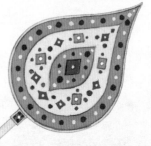

Servants waved large fans to keep the emperor cool. Find two fans.

Peacocks and monkeys roamed through the fort. Find ten peacocks and six monkeys.

Sometimes, poisonous snakes slipped into the courtyard. Spot nine snakes.

The palace artist painted pictures of important events. Can you spot the artist?

One mischievous monkey has stolen a turban ornament. Can you find it?

Can you see the prince who has come to visit the emperor?

The prince's courtiers carried ornaments on poles. See if you can find seven.

Visitors brought precious gifts for the emperor. Find four more gifts carried on cushions.

153

A romantic castle

Later castle-builders built 'fairy-tale' homes that looked like medieval castles but were much more comfortable. This picture shows inside a romantic castle, where a party is being held.

Huge banquets were prepared in the kitchen. Find the head cook.

Servants slept in small, plain rooms. Spot two servants' beds.

The castle had hot water for baths and flushing toilets. Find two toilets.

The castle roofs were topped by fancy weathervanes. Spot five more weathervanes.

Castle owners loved holding parties. Spot the king welcoming his guests.

Some guests waved to their friends arriving at the ball. Can you see 17 waving guests?

154

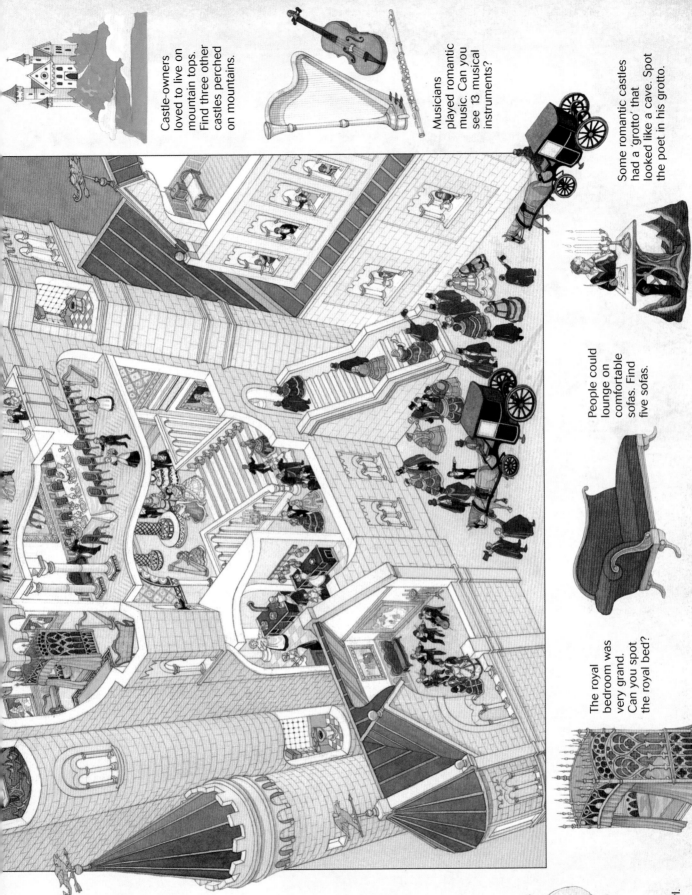

Castle-owners loved to live on mountain tops. Find three other castles perched on mountains.

Musicians played romantic music. Can you see 13 musical instruments?

Some romantic castles had a 'grotto' that looked like a cave. Spot the poet in his grotto.

People could lounge on comfortable sofas. Find five sofas.

The royal bedroom was very grand. Can you spot the royal bed?

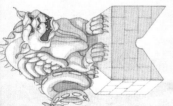

The castle had many dramatic carvings. Spot the stone dragon.

Oil paintings hung on the castle walls. Spot six oil paintings.

Food was served in beautiful dishes. Find the swan bowl.

155

Castle answers

The keys on the next few pages show you where to find all the people, animals and objects in the big scenes in this part of the book. You can use them to check your answers, or to help you if you have a problem finding anything.

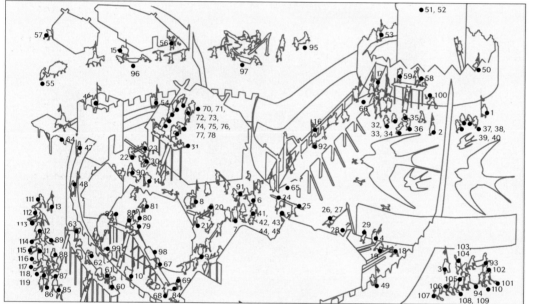

An early castle 134-135

Norman soldiers, 1, 2, 3, 4, 5, 6, 7, 8, 9, 10, 11, 12, 13, 14, 15, 16, 17

Carpenters sawing wood, 18, 19, 20, 21, 22, 23

Workers building palisade, 24, 25, 26, 27, 28, 29

Winch, 30

Falling Saxon, 31

Workers on lunch break, 32, 33, 34, 35, 36, 37, 38, 39, 40, 41, 42, 43, 44, 45

Lookouts, 46, 47, 48, 49, 50, 51, 52, 53, 54

Farm workers, 55, 56, 57

Builders applying limewash, 58, 59, 60, 61, 62, 63

Drawbridges, 64, 65, 66

Thatchers, 67, 68, 69, 70, 71, 72, 73, 74, 75, 76, 77, 78, 79, 80, 81, 82, 83

Stretchers, 84, 85, 86, 87, 88, 89, 90, 91, 92, 93, 94, 95

Sleds, 96, 97, 98

Hammers, 99, 100

Saxons with shovels, 101, 102, 103, 104, 105, 106, 107, 108, 109, 110, 111, 112, 113, 114, 115, 116, 117, 118, 119

In the great tower 136-137

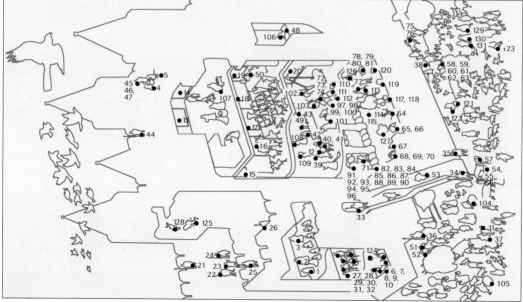

Priests, 1, 2, 3

Guards sharing snack, 4, 5

Prisoners, 6, 7, 8, 9, 10, 11, 12

Tapestries, 13, 14, 15, 16, 17, 18, 19, 20

Guards, 21, 22, 23, 24, 25, 26, 27, 28, 29, 30, 31, 32, 33, 34, 35, 36, 37, 38, 39, 40, 41, 42, 43, 44, 45, 46, 47, 48

Steward, 49

Lord, 50

Sacks, 51, 52, 53, 54, 55, 56, 57, 58, 59, 60, 61, 62, 63, 64, 65, 66, 67, 68, 69, 70, 71, 72, 73, 74, 75, 76, 77

Barrels, 78, 79, 80, 81, 82, 83, 84, 85, 86, 87, 88, 89, 90, 91, 92, 93, 94, 95, 96, 97, 98, 99, 100, 101, 102, 103, 104, 105

Guard on garderobe, 106

Lady working on tapestry, 107

Buckets, 108, 109, 110, 111, 112, 113, 114, 115, 116, 117, 118, 119, 120, 121, 122, 123, 124, 125, 126

Clerk, 127

Falling servant, 128

Merchants, 129, 130, 131

156

In the bailey 138-139

Carpenter making wheel, 1
Drying tunics, 2, 3, 4, 5, 6, 7, 8, 9
Cauldrons, 10, 11, 12, 13, 14, 15
Turnips, 16, 17, 18, 19, 20, 21, 22, 23, 24, 25
Milkmaids, 26, 27, 28
Loaves, 29, 30, 31, 32, 33, 34, 35, 36, 37, 38, 39, 40, 41, 42, 43, 44
Children playing ball, 45, 46, 47, 48, 49, 50, 51
Arrows, 52, 53, 54, 55, 56, 57, 58, 59, 60, 61, 62, 63, 64
Geese, 65, 66, 67, 68, 69, 70, 71
Farrier, 72
Stable boys, 73, 74, 75, 76, 77
Knife grinders, 78, 79, 80
Swords, 81, 82, 83, 84, 85, 86, 87, 88, 89, 90, 91, 92
Deer, 93, 94
Rabbits, 95, 96, 97, 98, 99, 100, 101, 102

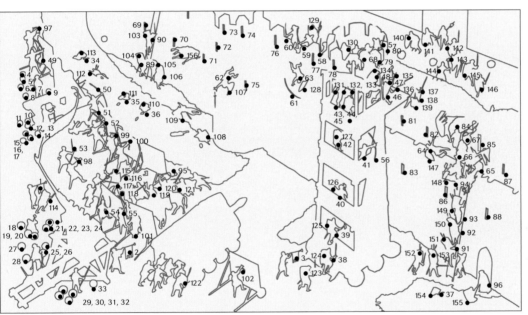

Under siege 140-141

Trumpeters, 1, 2, 3
Rocks, 4, 5, 6, 7, 8, 9, 10, 11, 12, 13, 14, 15, 16, 17, 18, 19, 20, 21, 22, 23, 24, 25, 26, 27, 28, 29, 30, 31, 32, 33
Swimmers, 34, 35, 36, 37
Men in siege tower, 38, 39, 40, 41, 42, 43, 44, 45, 46, 47, 48
Longbows, 49, 50, 51, 52, 53, 54, 55, 56, 57, 58, 59, 60, 61
Falling defenders, 62, 63, 64
Pots of fire, 65, 66, 67, 68
Arrow loops, 69, 70, 71, 72, 73, 74, 75, 76, 77, 78, 79, 80, 81, 82, 83, 84, 85, 86, 87, 88
Climbing or falling attackers, 89, 90, 91, 92, 93, 94
Morning star, 95
Spy, 96
Crossbows, 97, 98, 99 100, 101, 102
Shields, 103, 104, 105 106, 107, 108, 109, 110, 111, 112, 113, 114, 115, 116, 117, 118, 119, 120, 121, 122, 123, 124, 125, 126, 127, 128, 129, 130, 131, 132, 133, 134, 135, 136, 137, 138, 139, 140, 141, 142, 143, 144, 145, 146, 147, 148, 149, 150, 151, 152, 153, 154, 155
Flying cow, 156

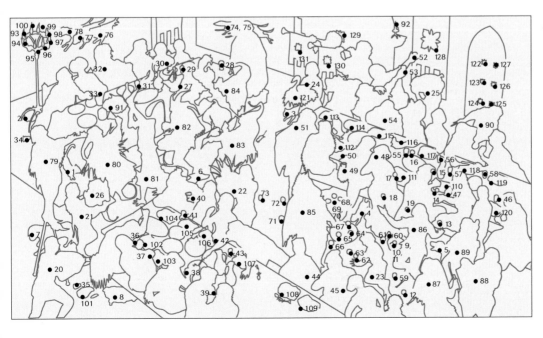

At a feast 142-143

Cats, 1, 2, 3, 4
Dogs, 5, 6, 7, 8
Juggling balls, 9, 10, 11, 12, 13, 14, 15, 16, 17, 18, 19
Servants, 20, 21, 22, 23, 24, 25
Marzipan castle, 26
Salt container, 27
Goblets, 28, 29, 30, 31, 32, 33, 34, 35, 36, 37, 38, 39, 40, 41, 42, 43, 44, 45, 46, 47, 48, 49, 50, 51, 52, 53, 54, 55, 56, 57, 58
Pies, 59, 60, 61, 62, 63, 64, 65, 66, 67, 68, 69, 70, 71, 72, 73
Dogs in tapestries, 74, 75, 76, 77, 78
Minstrels & entertainers, 79, 80, 81, 82, 83, 84, 85, 86, 87, 88, 89, 90
Boar's head, 91
Candles, 92, 93, 94, 95, 96, 97, 98, 99, 100
Bread slices, 101, 102, 103, 104, 105, 106, 107, 108, 109, 110, 111, 112, 113, 114, 115, 116, 117, 118, 119, 120
Stuffed swan, 121
Family emblems, 122, 123, 124, 125, 126, 127, 128, 129, 130, 131

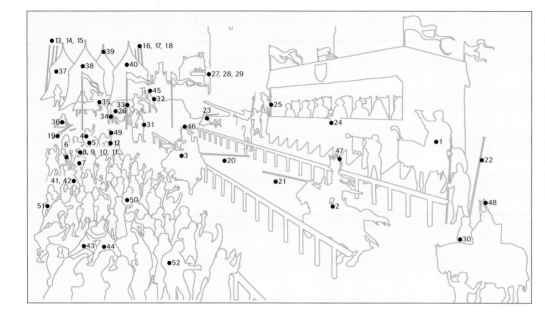

At a tournament 144-145

Herald, 1
Tokens, 2, 3,
Pies, 4, 5, 6, 7, 8, 9, 10, 11, 12
Lances, 13, 14, 15, 16, 17, 18, 19, 20, 21, 22
Jousting page, 23
Cup, 24
Climbing page, 25
Wounded knight, 26
Ladies on balcony, 27, 28, 29
Squires, 30, 31, 32, 33, 34, 35, 36
Pavillions, 37, 38, 39, 40
Wrestlers, 41, 42, 43, 44
Crests, 45, 46, 47, 48
Priests, 49, 50
Pickpockets, 51, 52

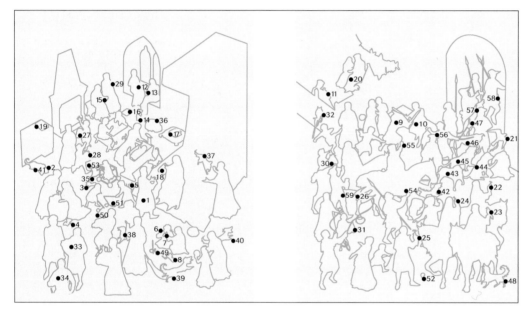

A family home 146-147

Cook, 1
Puppets, 2, 3, 4, 5, 6, 7, 8
Squires, 9, 10
Rattle, 11
Needlework, 12, 13, 14
Manuscripts, 15, 16, 17, 18, 19
Lord's mother, 20
Falcons, 21, 22, 23, 24, 25, 26
Hobby horses, 27, 28, 29, 30, 31, 32
Steward, 33
Constable, 34
Dogs, 35, 36, 37, 38, 39, 40, 41 42, 43, 44, 45, 46, 47, 48
Spinning tops, 49, 50, 51, 52
Chess piece, 53
Hunting horns, 54, 55, 56, 57, 58, 59

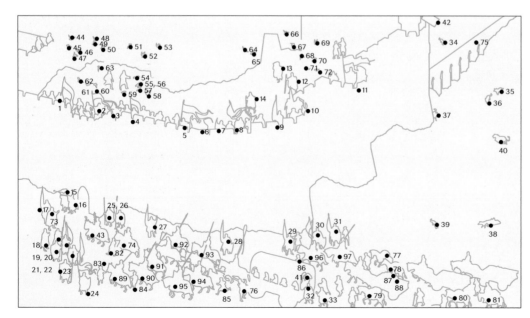

A crusader castle 148-149

Hospitaller knights, 1, 2, 3, 4, 5, 6, 7, 8, 9, 10, 11, 12, 13, 14, 15, 16, 17, 18, 19, 20, 21, 22, 23, 24, 25, 26, 27, 28, 29, 30, 31, 32, 33
Wolves, 34, 35, 36, 37, 38, 39
Lion, 40
Fainting lady, 41
Windmill, 42
King, 43
Pigeons, 44, 45, 46, 47, 48, 49, 50, 51, 52, 53, 54, 55, 56, 57, 58, 59, 60, 61, 62, 63, 64, 65, 66, 67, 68, 69, 70, 71, 72
Castellan, 73
Bishop, 74
Aqueduct, 75
Minstrel, 76
Mules, 77, 78, 79, 80, 81
Squires, 82, 83, 84, 85, 86, 87
Wounded knight, 88
Mounted knights, 89, 90, 91, 92, 93, 94, 95, 96, 97

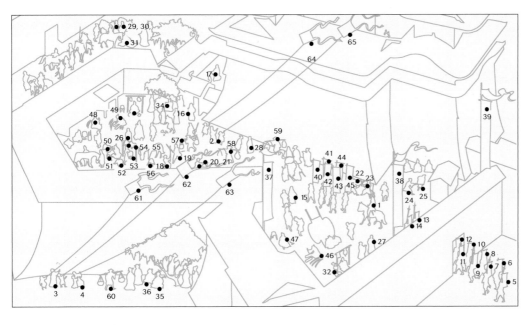

A samurai fortress 150-151

Daimyo, 1
Nursemaids, 2, 3, 4
Flags, 5, 6, 7, 8, 9, 10, 11, 12, 13, 14
Laundry baskets, 15, 16, 17
Samurai fighting with wooden swords, 18, 19, 20, 21, 22, 23, 24, 25
Priests, 26, 27, 28
Merchants, 29, 30, 31
Metalworkers, 32, 33
Poet, 34
Musicians, 35, 36
Banners, 37, 38, 39, 40, 41, 42, 43, 44, 45
Swordmakers, 46, 47, 48, 49
Saddles, 50, 51, 52, 53, 54, 55, 56
Farmers, 57, 58, 59, 60
Kites, 61, 62, 63, 64, 65

A Mogul fort 152-153

Emperor, 1,
Ladies, 2, 3, 4, 5, 6, 7, 8, 9, 10, 11, 12, 13, 14, 15, 16, 17, 18, 19, 20
Muskets, 21, 22, 23, 24
Drums, 25, 26, 27, 28
Horns, 29, 30, 31, 32, 33, 34, 35, 36, 37
Cymbals, 38, 39
Fans, 40, 41
Indian prince, 42
Ornaments on poles, 43, 44, 45, 46, 47, 48, 49
Gifts on cushions, 50, 51, 52, 53
Turban ornament, 54
Artist, 55
Snakes, 56, 57, 58, 59, 60, 61, 62, 63, 64
Peacocks, 65, 66, 67, 68, 69, 70, 71, 72, 73, 74
Monkeys, 75, 76, 77, 78, 79, 80

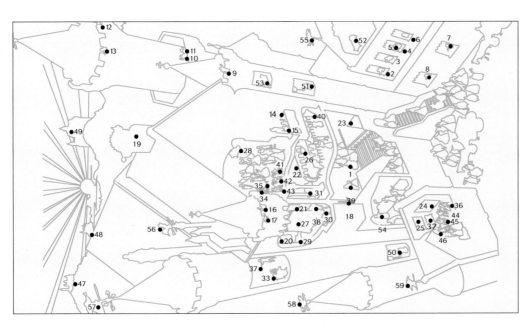

A romantic castle 154-155

King, 1
Waving guests, 2, 3, 4, 5, 6, 7, 8, 9, 10, 11, 12, 13, 14, 15, 16, 17, 18
Stone dragon, 19
Oil paintings, 20, 21, 22, 23, 24, 25
Swan bowl, 26
Royal bed, 27
Sofas, 28, 29, 30, 31, 32
Poet, 33
Cellos, 34, 35, 36
Flute, 37
Harps, 38, 39, 40
Violins, 41, 42, 43, 44, 45, 46
Castles, 47, 48, 49
Toilets, 50, 51
Servants' beds, 52, 53
Head cook, 54
Weathervanes, 55, 56, 57, 58, 59

Part Five

THE UNDERSEA SEARCH

This snake lives in the mangrove swamps. Find out what else lives there on pages 184 and 185

You can find penguins darting through the water off the Galapagos islands on pages 186 and 187.

Seabirds can dive deep to catch fish. Find these boobies on pages 186 and 187.

Learn about a diver's work on pages 182 and 183.

These undersea machines are used to repair oil rigs on pages 182 and 183.

Sea otters live in kelp forests. Find out who else lives there on pages 180 and 181.

Part Five

Many creatures that live in coral reefs have bright markings. You can find more of them on pages 178 and 179.

Find out about equipment that divers use underwater on pages 178 and 179.

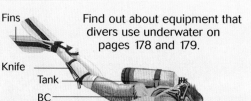

Fins

Knife

Tank

BC

Regulator

Discover which weird creatures live at the bottom of the sea on pages 176 and 177.

The Undersea Search

Ammonites lived over 200 million years ago. Find some other ancient creatures on pages 164 and 165.

In this part of the book you can find out about all sorts of exciting things that happen under the sea, and discover the animals and plants that live there. There are puzzles to solve too. This shows you how they work.

Find out where dangerous eels lurk on pages 166 and 167.

There are hundreds of things to find in each big picture. In real life the seas are much less crowded.

Around the outside of each big picture are lots of little ones.

The writing next to each picture tells you how many of that thing you can find in the big picture.

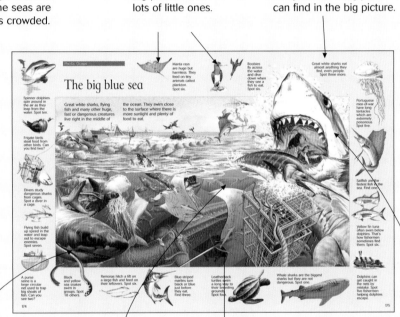

The big blue sea

Discover what you might find in pools among the rocks on pages 168 and 169.

Spot the first submarine to cross under the Arctic ice on pages 170 and 171.

You can only see part of this shark but it still counts.

This manta ray in the distance counts.

You will need to count all these snakes carefully.

This shark coming out of the picture is here instead of the little picture. You do not count it in your total.

The puzzle is to find all the things in the main picture. Some are easy, but others are tiny or partly hidden. Some animals look quite similar, so you will need to look carefully to spot the difference. If you can't find something, you can look up the answers on pages 188–191.

Find chests full of coins and more pirate treasure on pages 172 and 173.

Turn to pages 176 and 177 to find out about the submersibles that explore the ocean depths.

Sailfish are the fastest fish in the sea. You'll find them on pages 174 and 175.

Turn to pages 174 and 175 to find the most dangerous shark of all.

Prehistoric seas

Placodus had a very strong jaw. Find two.

Ammonites used their tentacles to catch food. Find 13.

Two hundred million years ago, dinosaurs ruled the land and giant creatures swam in the seas. Smaller ones lived there too. Some are still around today. Look closely to find 21 different creatures in this scene.

Banjo fish were ancient relatives of skates and rays. Can you see four more?

Ichthyosaurus gave birth under water. Find two adults and three babies.

Jellyfish lived up to 600 million years ago. Can you see four?

Giant sea turtles like archelon could hide inside their hard shells. Spot two.

Sea lilies are animals not flowers. Can you find a group of them?

Rabbit fish get their name from their funny faces. Find two.

Elasmosaurus had a really long neck. Find one.

Tanystropheus lived at the edge of the sea and ate fish. Find two.

Pliosaurus was fast and fierce. It could attack large creatures. Spot one.

As a belemnite grew, its shell grew longer. Can you find four more?

Sponges looked much the same as they do now. Find three groups.

Some people think the Loch Ness monster is a plesiosaurus. Find three.

Starfish

Sea urchins

Sea cucumber

These creatures moved slowly across the sea floor. Spot three of each.

There were lots of different sharks. Find three like this one.

Lampshells were attached to the seabed by stalks. Find two groups of them.

King crabs are still around today. They turn upside-down to swim. Spot two more.

Geosaurus had sharp teeth and a long snout. Find two.

Shipwreck

Some wrecks have hidden treasure. There are 18 gold bars to find here.

All parts of a wreck are soon covered with coral. Can you find the anchor?

Reef sharks look dangerous but they rarely attack divers. Find three.

This ship was carrying bikes. Can you find three covered with coral?

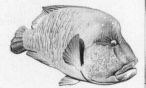

Napoleon wrasses are large, friendly fish which often follow divers. Spot three.

When you dive down to explore a wreck, you never know what you may find. There may be strange creatures lurking in the depths, or treasure buried in the sand. This ship sank years ago. Now it's covered in coral.

With an eye and a nostril on each side of its head, a hammerhead shark sees and smells well. Find four more.

Crocodile fish have shiny green eyes. Spot one hiding on the sea bed.

Corals of all shades grow on the wreck. Spot four pink clumps.

Parrot fish nibble the corals with their beak-like mouths. Spot three.

This diver is going down to explore the wreck. Can you find seven more?

Moray eels have very strong jaws. They hunt in the dark. Find four.

When they are scared, puffer fish blow up like spiky balloons. Can you see all four?

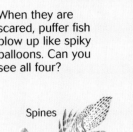

Spines

Lion fish have poisonous spines on their back. Spot two lion fish.

Cleaner fish clean the mouths and gills of larger fish. Spot four at work.

Blue spotted groupers like to live inside holes in the wreck. Find four.

These small fish recognize each other by their bright markings. Find 20 of each.

Angel fish

Anthias

Butterfly fish

Divers carry flashlights to see inside the darkest parts of a wreck. Spot four.

Glass fish swim around together in large groups called schools. Spot one school.

Common starfish

Cushion star

"Bloody Henry"

There are many types of starfish. Most have five arms. Spot four of each of these.

Beadlet anemones close up tightly to keep moist until the sea returns. Spot 20.

Hermit crabs live in empty shells. They move house as they grow. Can you find two?

Limpets

Mussels

Some animals that live in shells cling to the rocks. Find five groups of each of these.

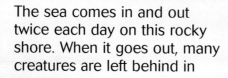

Rocky shore

Kittiwakes live on the cliffs and fish in the sea. Can you count 50?

The sea comes in and out twice each day on this rocky shore. When it goes out, many creatures are left behind in pools among the rocks like this one. If you look closely you will find over 100 creatures here.

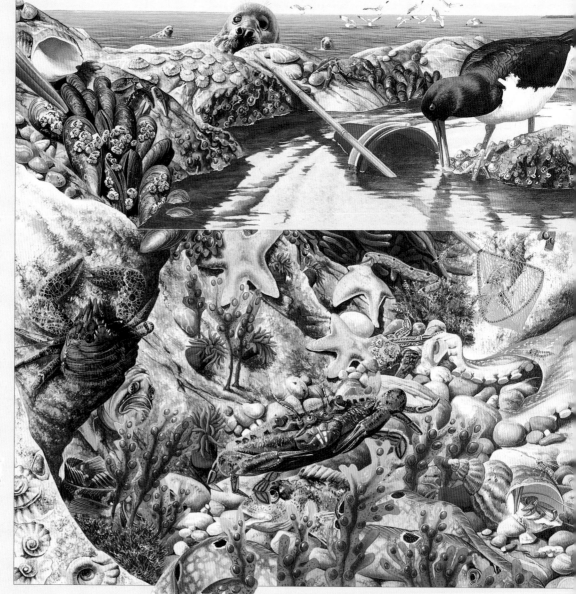

Grey seals have large eyes to see in cloudy water and thick fur to keep them warm. Spot nine.

Butterfish are long and thin with spots along their backs. Find four more.

With eyes on top of their heads, rock gobies can spot danger above. Find two.

Octopuses can squeeze into tiny spaces. Can you find one?

Some rocks have fossils like these ammonites in them. Find ten.

Oystercatchers use their sharp beaks to eat shellfish. Spot three more.

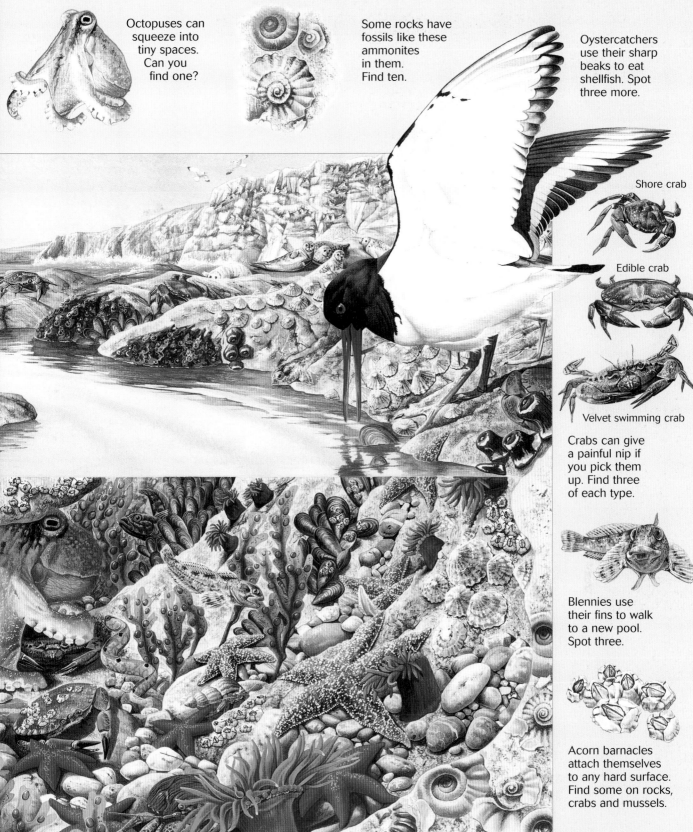

Shore crab

Edible crab

Velvet swimming crab

Crabs can give a painful nip if you pick them up. Find three of each type.

Blennies use their fins to walk to a new pool. Spot three.

Acorn barnacles attach themselves to any hard surface. Find some on rocks, crabs and mussels.

Prawns are hard to spot as they are almost transparent. Find seven.

Can you see a net and bucket that someone has left behind?

Squat lobsters have huge front legs that are bigger than their bodies. Spot two.

Bows

Icy seas

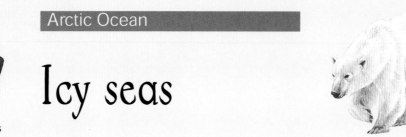

When polar bears swim, a layer of fat and thick fur keeps them warm in the icy water. Spot four.

Research ships have very strong bows to break through the ice. Spot one ship.

The Arctic Ocean is so cold that two-thirds of it is covered in ice all year round. Despite the freezing water, plenty of creatures live here. Scientists also visit to study the ice and learn about the world's changing climate.

Beluga whales are called "sea canaries" because they sing to each other. Spot three.

Baby seals are called pups. They have fluffy white coats. Spot three.

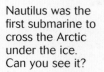

Nautilus was the first submarine to cross the Arctic under the ice. Can you see it?

Walruses can use their tusks to lever themselves out of the water. Find 15.

Scientists attach transmitters to some animals to find out how they live. Spot one.

Bearded seals use their long curly whiskers to find shellfish. Find three.

170

Male narwhals have a long spiral tusk that is actually a huge front tooth. Can you find eight?

Arctic terns fly from the very north to the very south of the world each year. Spot four.

Humpback whales sometimes leap right out of the water. Spot three.

Harp seal

Ringed seal

Ribbon seal

You can spot different seals by their markings. Find five of each of these.

Arctic skuas steal food from other birds. Spot two.

Puffins can use their wings like paddles to dive underwater for fish. Find three.

Killer whales catch seals by tipping up the ice so that they fall into the water. Spot three.

Little Auks gather in groups called rafts, while they look for food. Find ten.

Blue whales are probably the largest creatures that ever lived. Spot one.

Pirate treasure

Dolphin
handle

Find a gold cup
with dolphin
handles.

Pirates were
looking for
chests full of
coins. Spot
seven.

Hand
blower

Divers use hand
blowers to blow
away sand and
uncover treasure.
Spot two.

Barrel

Jar

Food for the
ship's crew was
stored in jars and
barrels like these.
Spot six of each.

Sometimes a
diver makes a
sketch of the
ship. Spot a
diver sketching.

In the 16th century, Spanish
ships called galleons sailed
from the Americas to Spain
laden with gold, silver and
jewels. Many were attacked
by pirates. These divers are
exploring a ship that sank
with all her treasure.

Musket

Sword

Dagger

The ship's
crew needed
weapons to fight
off the pirates.
Find two of each
of these.

Divers sometimes
use metal
detectors to
help find buried
treasures. Can
you see one?

Find two gold plates.

Dividers

Astrolabe

Sailors navigated by the sun and stars. Find these measuring instruments.

Sundial

Camera

When divers find a wreck, they measure and photograph it. Can you see a camera?

Grid

Heavy things are attached to lifting bags which float to the surface. Find eight.

Silver ingot

Gold ingot

Gold and silver from South America were made into ingots in Mexico. Find seven silver and six gold ingots.

Small objects are brought to the surface in baskets. Can you spot six?

Find some divers measuring part of the wreck.

Cannon

Cannonballs

The captain used this whistle to give orders to his crew. Can you find it?

Gold locket

Rich people sailed as passengers. Find these six jewels.

Rosary

Emerald cross

Buckle covered with jewels

Emerald ring

Gold chain

Galleons built for battle had lots of cannons. Can you find 10 cannons and 20 cannonballs?

173

The big blue sea

Manta rays are huge but harmless. They feed on tiny animals called plankton. Spot six.

Spinner dolphins spin around in the air as they leap from the water. Spot ten.

Frigate birds steal food from other birds. Can you find two?

Divers study dangerous sharks from cages. Spot a diver in a cage.

Flying fish build up speed in the water and leap out to escape enemies. Spot seven.

A purse seine is a large circular net used to trap big shoals of fish. Can you see two?

Great white sharks, flying fish and many other huge, fast or dangerous creatures live right in the middle of the ocean. They swim close to the surface where there is more sunlight and plenty of food to eat.

Black and yellow sea snakes swim in groups. Spot 18 others.

Remoras hitch a lift on large fish and feed on their leftovers. Spot six.

Blue-striped marlins turn black or blue just before they eat. Find three.

174

Boobies fly across the water and dive down when they see a fish to eat. Spot six.

Great white sharks eat almost anything they find, even people. Can you spot three more?

Portuguese men-of-war have long tentacles which are extremely poisonous. Spot five.

Sailfish are the fastest fish in the sea. Find one.

Yellow fin tuna often swim below dolphins. That's how fishermen sometimes find them. Spot six.

Dolphins can get caught in the nets by mistake. Spot five fishermen helping dolphins escape.

Leatherback turtles swim a long way to their breeding grounds. Spot four.

Whale sharks are the biggest sharks but they are not dangerous. Spot one.

175

The abyss

The very deepest part of the ocean, called the abyss, is icy cold and dark. Explorers go down in small submarines, called submersibles. They have found volcanoes, hot springs, deep trenches, and some very strange creatures.

Bathyscaphes look like huge airships. They go into deep trenches. Can you see two?

Angler fish use a long fin with a light on the end to catch other fish. Can you see three?

Beardworms grow huge on food from hot springs. Can you spot five groups of them?

Sonar "fish" are towed by ships. They record what's on the ocean floor. Spot three.

Tripod fish walk along the sea floor on long fins like legs. Find one.

176

Nautile

Alvin

Turtle

Submersibles need thick walls, to stop the water above from crushing them. Spot each of these.

Deep sea spiders can be 50cm (20in) across. Can you see five?

Hatchet fish have two huge eyes on top of their heads. Spot 17.

Giant squid have huge eyes that are about 17 times the size of yours. Spot four.

Anemone

Vent fish

Crab

These strange creatures live and feed around the smokers. Find 20 of each.

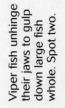

Deep Flight is a submersible that can fly to the bottom fast. Can you see it?

Viper fish unhinge their jaws to gulp down large fish whole. Spot two.

Lantern fish have lights all along their bodies. Find 22.

Submersibles and ROVs have manipulator arms for picking things up. Spot five more.

Gulper eels swallow large fish with their wide mouths. Spot four.

Sperm whales dive deep for food, but they must swim to the surface to breathe. Can you find two?

ROVs are controlled by a cable from submersibles or ships. Can you see three?

Tall chimneys called black smokers grow up around hot springs. Can you find 15?

177

Coral dives

Millions of people dive for fun, and Australia's Great Barrier Reef is one of the best places to explore.

The reef is made from the skeletons of billions of tiny creatures called corals. Can you find 15 divers here?

Sea slugs are small but they have bright markings. Spot each of these.

Flash light

Underwater cameras need strong flash lights. Can you see four?

Sea wasp

Cone shell

Olive sea snake

These creatures are so poisonous, they can kill a person. Find one of each.

Fins help divers swim smoothly. Spot three yellow pairs.

Giant clams grow very slowly and can live for 100 years. Can you find two?

Tank

Regulator

Divers breathe compressed air from tanks. Spot a diver with two tanks.

Snorkel

Can you find three blue snorkels?

Mask

Can you find a leaking mask, half full of water?

"Let's go up"

"I'm OK"

Divers use hand signals to "talk" to each other. Spot two divers making each of these signals.

Sea fan

Staghorn coral

Brain coral

Corals are animals though some look more like rocks. Spot four clumps of each type.

Divers wear weights on their belts to help them descend. Find a diver with six weights.

Clown fish hide in poisonous anemones. Find nine others.

Barracudas are curious and sometimes follow a diver. Spot five.

Divers add air to jackets called BCs to go up, and let it out to go down. Spot a pink BC.

Hundreds of small fish live in the reef. Find three of each of these.

Surgeon fish

Clown Triggerfish

Moorish idol

Can you find four divers with knives?

Knife

Wetsuit

Can you see a diver in a short pink wetsuit like this one?

Depth gauge

Air

Consoles with dials show how much air is left and how deep it is. Find four.

Marker buoys on the surface show where the divers are. Can you see one?

179

Kelp forest

Californian coast, USA

Giant kelp is the fastest growing plant in the world. It can grow 60cm (24in) in a day. Huge underwater kelp forests are home to thousands of creatures. People use the kelp too, to make things such as ice cream or paint.

As kelp crabs get bigger, they shed their shell and grow a new one. Spot six.

Sea stars stand on tiptoe to shed their eggs. Can you find two?

Bat rays glide through the forest on wing-like fins. Can you see three?

Ocean goldfish guard their space in the kelp fiercely. Find 11.

Sea otters wrap up in kelp when they snooze on the surface. Find eight.

Gray whales shelter in the kelp to keep their babies safe. Spot a mother and her baby.

Sea snails eat their way up kelp plants. Spot 17.

Californian sealions are speedy swimmers and like to play. Spot three.

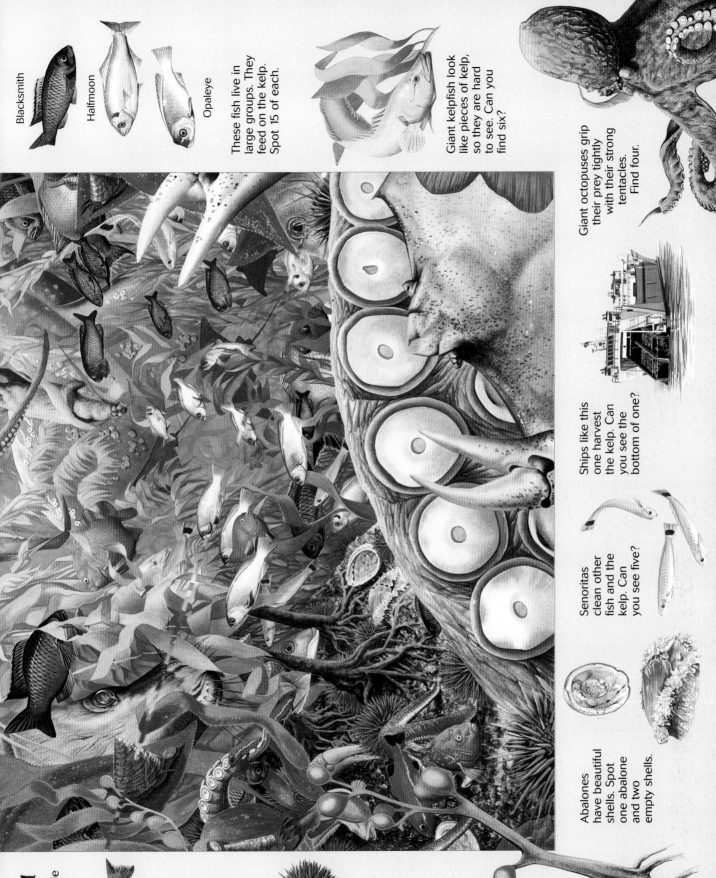

Blacksmith

Halfmoon

Opaleye

These fish live in large groups. They feed on the kelp. Spot 15 of each.

Giant kelpfish look like pieces of kelp, so they are hard to see. Can you find six?

Giant octopuses grip their prey tightly with their strong tentacles. Find four.

Ships like this one harvest the kelp. Can you see the bottom of one?

Senoritas clean other fish and the kelp. Can you see five?

Abalones have beautiful shells. Spot one abalone and two empty shells.

Young

Female

Male

Male, female and young sheephead wrasses all look different. Spot three of each.

Hungry sea urchins destroy the kelp. Find six red and six purple ones.

Each kelp plant has a holdfast which clings to the rock. Spot three more.

Oil rigs

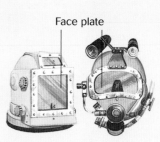

Face plate

Helmets let divers see and breathe easily. Find one with a square face plate.

Rigs are built on land and then towed out to sea. Can you find five of them?

When oil is found beneath the sea, giant rigs are built to bring it to the surface. Underwater machines, called ROVs, and deep sea divers check the rigs for damage and do repairs. It can be dangerous work.

Newtsuit

Hard suits stop the water pushing in on the diver. The Newtsuit has legs with special joints. Find two.

Wasp suit

Wasp suits have propellers to help them move around. Can you find five?

Conger eels have sharp teeth. They live in holes, so divers have to watch where they put their hands. Spot four.

Diving bells are used to lower divers into deep water. Can you find three?

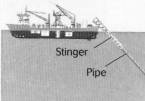

Pipe-laying barge

Stinger

Pipe

Pipes are laid by these special barges. Find one.

Special rods are heated up to cut metal. Spot three divers cutting.

Some seals are fierce and try to chase divers away. Spot five.

Diving support vessel

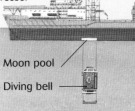

Moon pool

Diving bell

Diving equipment is lowered into the water from a diving support vessel. Find one.

Diver in hardsuit

Airbags are used to support heavy things in the water. Spot ten.

Tools are lowered from the surface in these baskets. Find five.

Work ROV

Different types of ROVs (remotely operated vehicles) are used for each job. Work ROVs have mechanical arms. Spot three.

Eyeball ROVs have cameras which film any damage and repairs. Spot six.

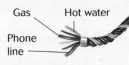

Gas   Hot water

Phone line

Umbilicals join divers to a bell, bringing them hot water and gas. Spot six.

Mussels grow all over the rig and sometimes have to be cleaned off. Spot five groups of them.

Find 12 of each of these fish.

Pollack

Cod

Water jet pumps are used for tasks such as cleaning. Can you see one?

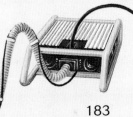

Seaside jungle

Ospreys catch fish with their large feet and claws. Spot one.

A glossy ibis uses its long beak to catch shellfish, insects and even snakes. Spot four.

The tangled roots of mangrove trees make a perfect home for many different creatures. These trees grow in hot parts of the world where a river meets the sea. Their roots reach down into the water to help prop them up.

Otters paddle on the surface and dive down for food. Find three.

Soldier crabs can recognize each other by their blue shells. Spot 22.

Saltwater crocodiles are very dangerous and very large. Find three more.

Dog-headed sea snakes slither through the water hunting for fish and crabs. Spot seven.

Mudskippers can use their fins like arms to drag themselves along the mud. Spot 25.

Oyster

Chama

The mangrove roots are a good place for shellfish to breed. Spot 21 of each of these.

Young tripletail fish hide on their sides near the surface. They look like dead leaves. Spot 12.

Ocean creatures often visit the mangroves to feed on plants. Can you spot two turtles?

Crab-eating macaques use their strong teeth to open shellfish. Spot two more.

When kingfishers spot a fish, they plunge head first after it. Find five.

Proboscis monkeys like to swim. They often dive into the water to cool off. Spot five.

Some mangrove seedlings float for a year before planting themselves in the mud. Find 14.

Unlike most frogs, crab-eating frogs are happy in salt water. Can you spot three?

Male fiddler crabs use their enormous claw to fight off rivals. Find three.

185

Volcanic islands

A few of these volcanic islands are still erupting. Can you see one?

Sealions surf in the waves for fun, but must watch out for sharks. Find five.

Flightless cormorants hold their little wings out to dry after a dive. Spot one.

Common dolphin

Spotted dolphin

Dolphins come to the surface frequently for air. Find two of each of these types.

Spot four swallow-tailed gulls.

The Galápagos islands were formed by volcanoes erupting at the bottom of the sea. They are a long way from any other land. Some creatures that live here are found nowhere else in the world.

Pelicans scoop up fish in the pouch under their beaks. Spot two.

Squid have two long arms and eight short ones. Find three.

A male frigate bird blows up his throat pouch to attract a mate. Spot two.

186

Pilot whales nudge their babies to the surface to breathe. Spot a mother and baby.

Albatrosses live mostly at sea. They only come to land to breed. Find one.

Fur seals get too hot in the midday sun, so they lie in the water to cool off. Spot two.

Red-footed booby

Blue-footed booby

Boobies make spectacular dives from 25m (82ft) high. Find four of each.

Sally lightfoot crabs have red shells and blue bellies. Spot 25.

These penguins use their stubby wings to "fly" through the water. Spot eight.

Tiger sharks hunt alone. They swim all day, only stopping to eat. Can you find one?

Marine iguanas are lizards that can swim. They have to lie in the sun to warm up. Find 14 more.

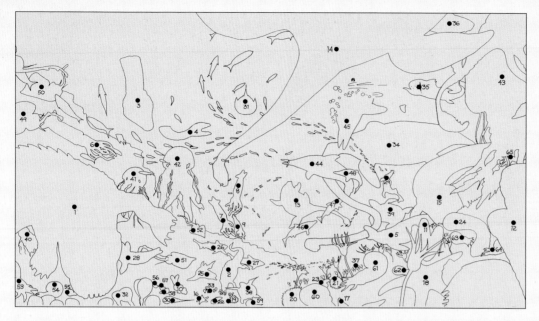

Prehistoric seas 164–165

Placodus 1 2
Tanystropheus 3 4
Pliosaurus 5
Belemnites 6 7 8 9
Sponges 10 11 12
Plesiosaurus 13
  14 15
Starfish 16 17 18
Sea urchins 19
  20 21
Sea cucumbers 22
  23 24
Sharks 25 26 27
Geosaurus 28 29
King crabs 30 31
Lampshells 32 33
Elasmosaurus 34
Rabbit fish 35 36
Sea lilies 37
Archelon 38 39
Jellyfish 40 41
  42 43
Ichthyosaurus:
  adults 44 45
  babies 46 47 48

Banjo fish 49 50
  51 52
Ammonites 53
  54 55 56 57 58
  59 60 61 62 63
  64 65

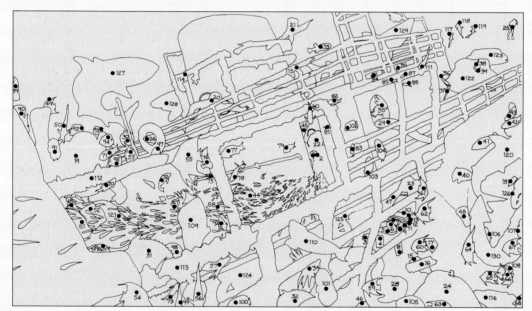

Shipwreck 166–167

Gold bars 1 2 3 4 5
  6 7 8 9 10 11 12
  13 14 15 16 17 18
Divers 19 20 21 22
  23 24 25
Moray eels 26 27
  28 29
Puffer fish 30 31
  32 33
Lion fish 34 35
Cleaner fish 36 37
  38 39
Blue spotted
groupers 40 41
  42 43
Glass fish 44
Flashlights 45 46
  47 48
Angel fish 49 50 51
  52 53 54 55 56
  57 58 59 60 61
  62 63 64 65 66
  67 68
Anthias 69 70 71
  72 73 74 75 76
  77 78 79 80 81
  82 83 84 85 86

87 88
Butterfly fish 89 90
  91 92 93 94 95
  96 97 98 99 100
  101 102 103 104
  105 106 107 108
Parrot fish 109
  110 111
Pink corals 112 113
  114 115
Crocodile fish 116
Hammerhead sharks
  117 118 119 120
Napoleon wrasses
  121 122 123
Bikes 124 125 126
Reef sharks 127 128
  129
Anchor 130

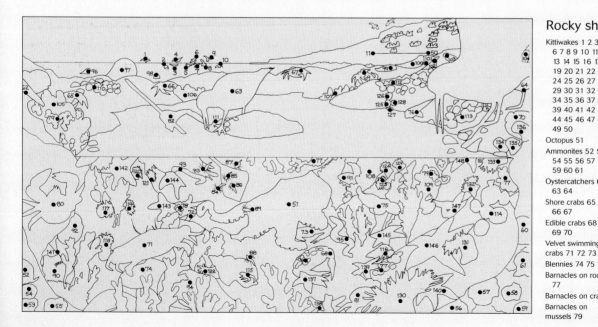

Rocky shore 168–169

Kittiwakes 1 2 3 4 5
  6 7 8 9 10 11 12
  13 14 15 16 17 18
  19 20 21 22 23
  24 25 26 27 28
  29 30 31 32 33
  34 35 36 37 38
  39 40 41 42 43
  44 45 46 47 48
  49 50
Octopus 51
Ammonites 52 53
  54 55 56 57 58
  59 60 61
Oystercatchers 62
  63 64
Shore crabs 65
  66 67
Edible crabs 68
  69 70
Velvet swimming
crabs 71 72 73
Blennies 74 75 76
Barnacles on rocks
  77
Barnacles on crabs 78
Barnacles on
mussels 79

Squat lobsters 80 81
Net and bucket 82
Prawns 83 84 85 86
  87 88 89
Rock gobies 90 91
Butterfish 92 93
  94 95
Grey seals 96 97 98
  99 100 101 102
  103 104
Mussels 105 106
  107 108 109
Limpets 110 111 112
  113 114
Hermit crabs 115 116
Beadlet anemones
  117 118 119 120
  121 122 123 124
  125 126 127 128
  129 130 131 132
  133 134 135 136
"Bloody Henry"
starfish 137 138
  139 140
Cushion star 141 142
  143 144
Common starfish
  145 146 147 148

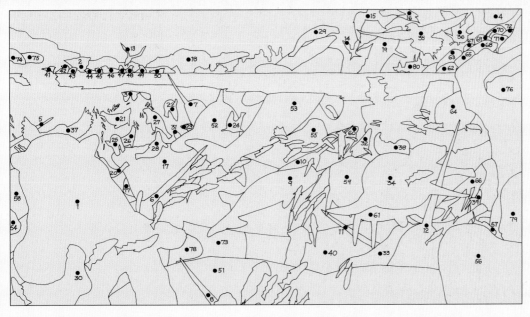

Icy seas 170–171

Polar bears 1 2 3 4
Narwhals 5 6 7 8 9
  10 11 12
Arctic terns 13 14
  15 16
Humpback whales
  17 18
Harp seals 19 20 21
  22 23 24
Ringed seals 25 26
  27 28 29
Ribbon seals 30 31
  32 33 34
Arctic skuas 35 36
Puffins 37 38 39
Blue whale 40
Little auks 41 42 43
  44 45 46 47 48
  49 50
Killer whales 51
  52 53
Bearded seals 54
  55 56
Transmitter 57
Walruses 58 59 60
  61 62 63 64 65

66 67 68 69 70
  71 72
Nautilus 73
Baby seals 74 75 76
Beluga whales 77
  78 79
Research ship 80

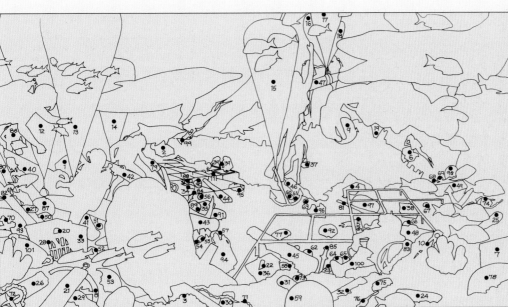

Pirate treasure 172–173

Chest of coins 1 2 3
  4 5 6 7
Astrolabe 8
Sundial 9
Dividers 10
Camera 11
Lifting bags 12 13 14
  15 16 17 18 19
Gold ingots 20 21
  22 23 24 25
Silver ingots 26 27
  28 29 30 31 32
Baskets 33 34 35
  36 37 38
Divers measuring 39
Cannons 40 41 42
  43 44 45 46 47
  48 49
Cannonballs 50 51
  52 53 54 55 56
  57 58 59 60 61
  62 63 64 65 66
  67 68 69
Emerald cross 70
Gold chain 71
Rosary 72

Emerald ring 73
Gold locket 74
Buckle 75
Whistle 76
Gold plates 77 78
Metal detector 79
Muskets 80 81
Swords 82 83
Daggers 84 85
Diver sketching 86
Jars 87 88 89 90
  91 92
Barrels 93 94 95 96
  97 98
Hand blowers 99
  100
Gold cup 101

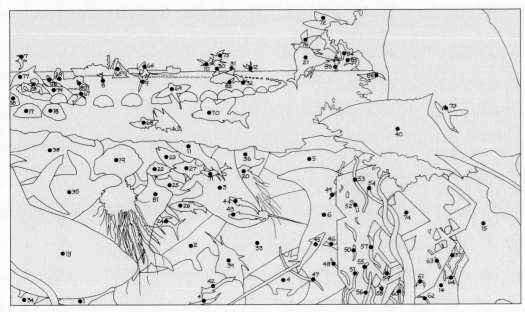

The big blue sea 174–175

Manta rays 1 2 3 4
  5 6
Boobies 7 8 9 10
  11 12
Great white sharks
  13 14 15
Portuguese men-
of-war 16 17 18
  19 20
Sailfish 21
Yellow fin tuna 22
  23 24 25 26 27
Fishermen 28 29 30
  31 32
Whale shark 33
Leatherback turtles
  34 35 36 37
Marlins 38 39 40
Remoras 41 42 43
  44 45 46
Sea snakes 47
  48 49 50 51 52
  53 54 55 56 57
  58 59 60 61 62
  63 64
Purse seine nets
  65 66

Flying fish 67 68 69
  70 71 72 73
Diver in cage 74
Frigate birds 75 76
Spinner dolphins 77
  78 79 80 81 82
  83 84 85 86

189

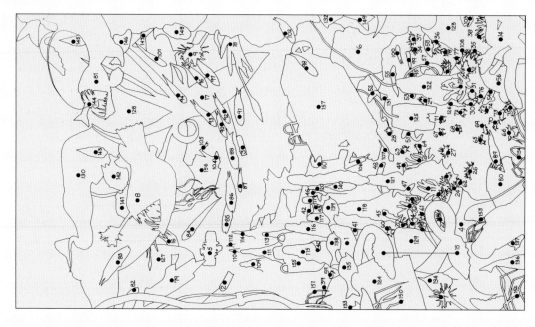

The abyss 176–177

Sonar "fish" 1 2 3
Tripod fish 4
Bathyscaphes 5 6
Angler fish 7 8 9
Beardworms 10 11
  12 13 14
Giant squid 15 16
  17 18
Anemones 19 20 21
  22 23 24 25 26
  27 28 29 30 31
  32 33 34 35 36
  37 38
Vent fish 39 40 41
  42 43 44 45 46
  47 48 49 50 51
  52 53 54 55 56
  57 58
Crabs 59 60 61
  62 63 64 65 66
  67 68 69 70 71
  72 73 74 75 76
  77 78
Deep Flight 79
Viper fish 80 81
Lantern fish 82
  83 84 85 86 87
  88 89 90 91 92

93 94 95 96 97
  98 99 100 101
  102 103
Manipulator arms
  104 105 106
  107 108
Black smokers 109
  110 111 112 113
  114 115 116 117
  118 119 120 121
  122 123
ROVs 124 125 126
Sperm whales 127
  128
Gulper eels 129 130
  131 132
Hatchet fish 133 134
  135 136 137 138
  139 140 141 142
  143 144 145 146
  147 148 149
Deep sea spiders
  150 151 152
  153 154
Submersibles:
  Turtle 155
  Alvin 156
  Nautile 157

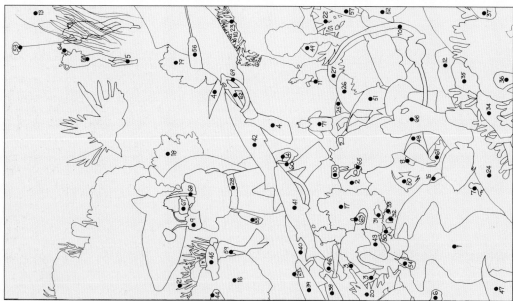

Coral dives 178–179

Giant clams 1 2
Yellow fins 3 4 5
Sea slugs 6 7 8
Cameras 9 10 11 12
Sea wasp 13
Olive sea snake 14
Cone shell 15
Coral:
  Sea fan 16 17
    18 19
  Staghorn 20 21
    22 23
  Brain 24 25 26 27
Diver with six
  weights 28
Clown fish 29 30
  31 32 33 34 35
  36 37
Barracudas 38 39
  40 41 42
Pink BC 43
Clown triggerfish 44
  45 46
Surgeon fish 47
  48 49

Moorish idol 50
  51 52
Marker buoy 53
Consoles 54 55
  56 57
Diver in short pink
  wetsuit 58
Knives 59 60 61 62
Divers' signals:
  "Let's go up"
    63 64
  "I'm OK" 65 66
Leaking mask 67
Blue snorkels 68
  69 70
Diver with two tanks
  71

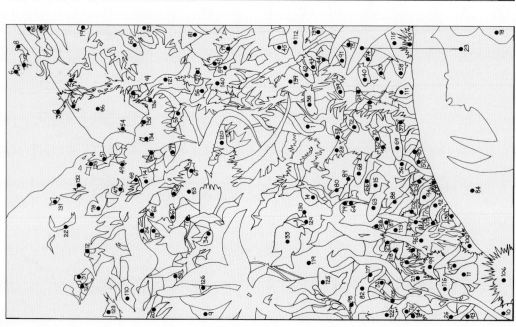

Kelp forest 180–181

Sea otters 1 2 3 4 5
  6 7 8
Ocean goldfish 9 10
  11 12 13 14 15 16
  17 18 19
Kelp crabs 20 21 22
  23 24 25
Sea stars 26 27
Bat rays 28 29 30
Blacksmiths 31 32
  33 34 35 36 37
  38 39 40 41 42
  43 44 45
Halfmoons 46 47 48
  49 50 51 52 53
  54 55 56 57 58
  59 60
Opaleyes 61 62 63
  64 65 66 67 68
  69 70 71 72 73
  74 75
Giant kelpfish 76 77
  78 79 80 81
Giant octopuses 82
  83 84 85
Ship 86
Senoritas 87 88 89
  90 91

Abalone 92
Empty abalone shells
  93 94
Holdfasts 95 96 97
Red sea urchins 98
  99 100 101 102
  103
Purple sea urchins
  104 105 106 107
  108 109
Sheephead wrasses:
  male 110 111 112
  female 113 114 115
  young 116 117 118
Sealions 119
  120 121
Sea snails 122 123
  124 125 126 127
  128 129 130 131
  132 133 134 135
  136 137 138
Gray whales:
  mother 139
  baby 140

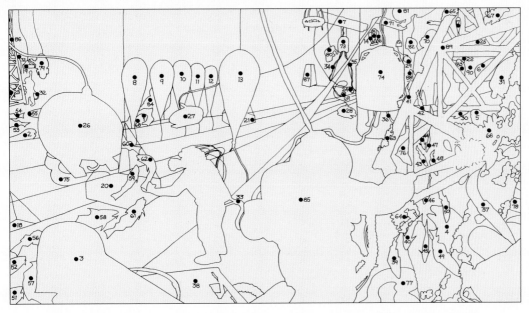

Oil rigs 182–183

Helmet with square face plate 1
Seals 2 3 4 5 6
Diving support vessel 7
Airbags 8 9 10 11 12 13 14 15 16 17
Tool baskets 18 19 20 21 22
Work ROVs 23 24 25
Eyeball ROVs 26 27 28 29 30 31
Umbilicals 32 33 34 35 36 37
Water jet pump 38
Pollack 39 40 41 42 43 44 45 46 47 48 49 50
Cod 51 52 53 54 55 56 57 58 59 60 61 62
Mussels 63 64 65 66 67
Divers cutting 68 69 70

Pipe-laying barge 71
Diving bells 72 73 74
Conger eels 75 76 77 78
Wasp suits 79 80 81 82 83
Newtsuits 84 85
Rigs 86 87 88 89 90

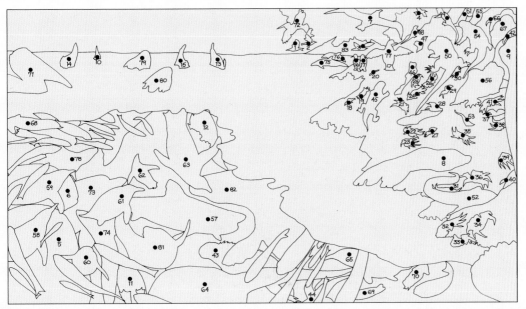

Seaside jungle 184–185

Osprey 1
Tripletail fish 2 3 4 5 6 7 8 9 10 11 12 13
Turtles 14 15
Crab-eating macaques 16 17
Kingfishers 18 19 20 21 22
Proboscis monkeys 23 24 25 26 27
Male fiddler crabs 28 29 30
Crab-eating frogs 31 32 33
Mangrove seedlings 34 35 36 37 38 39 40 41 42 43 44 45 46 47
Oysters 48 49 50 51 52 53 54 55 56 57 58 59 60 61 62 63 64 65 66 67 68

Chama 69 70 71 72 73 74 75 76 77 78 79 80 81 82 83 84 85 86 87 88 89
Mudskippers 90 91 92 93 94 95 96 97 98 99 100 101 102 103 104 105 106 107 108 109 110 111 112 113 114
Dog-headed sea snakes 115 116 117 118 119 120 121
Saltwater crocodiles 122 123 124
Soldier crabs 125 126 127 128 129 130 131 132 133 134 135 136 137 138 139 140 141 142 143 144 145 146
Otters 147 148 149
Glossy ibis 150 151 152 153

Volcanic islands 186–187

Swallow-tailed gulls 1 2 3 4
Pilot whale:
adult 5
baby 6
Albatross 7
Fur seals 8 9
Red-footed boobies 10 11 12 13
Blue-footed boobies 14 15 16 17
Sally lightfoot crabs 18 19 20 21 22 23 24 25 26 27 28 29 30 31 32 33 34 35 36 37 38 39 40 41 42
Marine iguanas 43 44 45 46 47 48 49 50 51 52 53 54 55 56
Tiger shark 57
Penguins 58 59 60 61 62 63 64 65
Male frigate birds 66 67

Squid 68 69 70
Pelicans 71 72
Spotted dolphins 73 74
Common dolphins 75 76
Cormorant 77
Sealions 78 79 80 81 82
Volcanic island erupting 83

191

Part Six

THE
BUG
SEARCH

Contents

The Bug Search

This part of the book is all about bugs. If you look hard, you'll find beetles, butterflies, spiders, slugs, snails, and hundreds of other creepy-crawlies from all around the world. This is how the puzzles work.

Some bugs live around our homes. Find out which ones on pages 196 and 197.

See inside these trapdoor spiders' burrows in the desert on pages 198 and 199.

This cockroach from Madagascar makes an odd noise. Find out more on pages 200 and 201.

There are about 100 bugs in each big picture. In real life, there wouldn't be as many in one place at the same time.

Around the outside of each big picture, there are lots of little pictures.

The writing next to each little picture tells you how many of that bug to look for in the big picture.

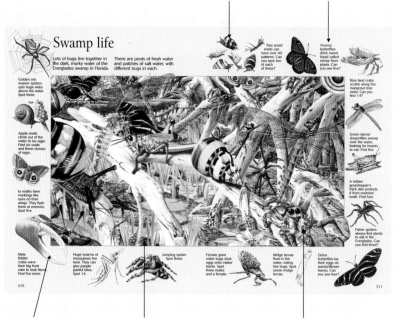

Swamp life

Lots of bugs live together in the dark, murky water of the Everglades swamp in Florida.

There are pools of fresh water and patches of salt water, with different bugs in each.

Tree snails' shells can have over 40 patterns. Can you spot two of each of these?

Viceroy butterflies drink sweet liquid called nectar from plants. Can you see five?

Golden orb weaver spiders spin huge webs above the water. Spot three.

Blue land crabs scuttle along the mangrove tree roots. Can you find 14?

Apple snails climb out of the water to lay eggs. Find six snails and three clumps of eggs.

Green darner dragonflies swoop over the water, looking for insects to eat. Find five.

Io moths have markings like eyes on their wings. They flash them at enemies. Spot five.

A lubber grasshopper's thick skin protects it from enemies' teeth. Find four.

Fisher spiders always find plenty to eat in the Everglades. Can you find five?

Male fiddler crabs wave their big front claw to look fierce. Find five more.

Huge swarms of mosquitoes live here. They can give people painful bites. Spot 14.

Jumping spider. Spot three.

Female giant water bugs stick eggs onto males' backs. Spot three males and a female.

Midge larvae float in the water, eating tiny bugs. Spot seven midge larvae.

Zebra butterflies lay their eggs on passionflower leaves. Can you see four?

210   211

This crab coming out of the big picture counts as a little picture too.

This part of a snail's shell counts as one snail.

A spider is about to eat this mosquito, but the mosquito still counts.

Some of the bugs are very easy to spot, but some are tiny, or hidden against their background. If you get really stuck, you'll find all the answers on pages 220–223.

On pages 202 and 203, you can find out why you should steer clear of these wandering spiders from Peru.

These pretty emperor gum moths live among the eucalyptus trees in Australia. See what else does on pages 204 and 205.

Worker bees have busy lives. Find out about the jobs they do in a beehive on page 217.

Queen termites are much bigger than any other termites. On page 216, you can see a queen inside her home.

In South Africa, assassin bugs can be dangerous. You'll discover why on pages 214 and 215.

Hidden extras

You'll find one of these animals hiding on each page. On pages split into two halves (pages 200–201, 212–213 and 216–217), there's one animal in each half.

Aardvark

Orang-utan

Mouse

Blue tree boa

Green tree frog

Kudu

Ring-tailed lemur

Hedgehog

Bandicoot

Great white heron

Cat

Tapir

Alligator

Burrowing owl

Hairy bird-eating spiders live deep in the jungle. Find out more about them on pages 212 and 213.

Young bugs

Young bugs are often called nymphs or larvae. They may look very different from their parents. Here's how a dragonfly grows up.

Adult flying

Dragonflies lay eggs in or near water. Each egg hatches into a dragonfly nymph.

Nymph

As it grows, the nymph loses its skin. The last time it does this, it becomes an adult.

Adult emerging

Lubber grasshoppers live in the Everglades swamp in the USA. You'll find them on pages 210 and 211.

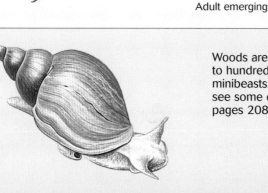

Pond snails make life easier for all the animals living in a pond. Find out how on pages 206 and 207.

Woods are home to hundreds of different minibeasts. You can see some of them on pages 208 and 209.

Homes and gardens

Not all minibeasts live in wild places. Many live in gardens, parks, and even in and around houses. This is a picture of a house in Britain. Can you spot 158 creatures here?

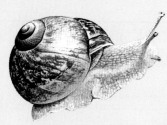

Snails leave sticky trails which show where they have been. Can you track down ten?

Most fleas drink the blood of animals. Some also drink human blood. Spot ten.

Female garden spiders are bigger than males and often eat them after mating. Spot eight spiders.

Houseflies' mouths are like a mop, soaking up liquid food. Find ten houseflies.

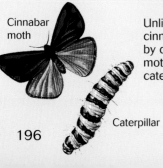

Cinnabar moth

Caterpillar

Unlike most moths, cinnabar moths fly by day. Spot seven moths and six caterpillars.

Lacewings sleep somewhere warm all winter. They turn brown while they sleep. Find 14.

Cockroaches have flat bodies. They can squeeze under things to hide. Spot 11.

Male

Female common blue butterfly

Only male common blue butterflies are really blue. Spot four of each sex.

Honeybees carry yellow pollen from flowers in "baskets" on their back legs. Can you find ten?

Zebra spiders creep up behind their victims and pounce on them. Find five.

Their name means "100 feet" but no centipedes have that many. Can you spot six?

Wasps like anything sweet, including our food. They'll sting you if you annoy them. Spot 13.

Devil's coach-horses arch their bodies to scare off enemies. Spot six coach-horses.

Earwigs lift their fierce-looking tails if they are scared, but they can't hurt you. Spot nine.

Tail

Greenflies suck the juice out of plants for their food. Can you spot 17?

Spittle bugs blow air and spit out of their bottoms to make foam. Find eight bugs hidden in foam.

Cactus city

This dry desert in the north of Mexico doesn't look like a very comfortable home, but thousands of bugs live here. Many stay in cool underground burrows during the hot day.

Some people keep Mexican red-kneed bird-eating spiders as pets. Can you find four here?

Painted grasshoppers are named after their bright-looking bodies. Can you spot ten?

Harvester ants collect seeds and store them deep underground. Find 15 busy ants.

Hercules beetles are some of the biggest insects in the world. Can you spot six?

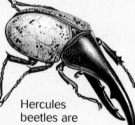

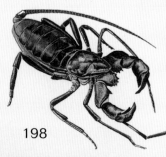

Whip scorpions have a long, thin tail like a whip. It can't hurt you, though. Spot five.

Ant-lion larvae dig pits in the sand. When other bugs fall in, they eat them. Find three.

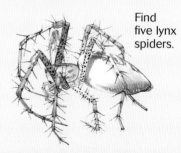

Find five lynx spiders.

Tarantula hawk wasps lay their eggs on tarantula spiders' bodies. Can you find seven of them?

When insects pass a trapdoor spider's home, it flips up its "door" and grabs them. Spot four.

Scorpions lurk in cool burrows until the sun sets. Then they go hunting. Spot six.

Giant red velvet mites hatch out after rain and rush around looking for food. Spot ten.

Some honey ants hang upside down in the nest. Their tummies are full of honey. Spot 13.

Blister beetles sting your skin if you touch them. Find four blister beetles.

Yucca moths only lay their eggs in a yucca plant's flowers. Spot five yucca moths.

Tarantula. Find six.

A southern black widow spider will only bite you if you annoy it. Can you spot four?

Island paradise

The island of Madagascar is home to many bugs that aren't found anywhere else. The bugs on this page live in thick, dry woods. Those on the opposite page live in a rainforest.

Brilliant red dragonflies flit through the trees in the rainforest. Spot four.

Striped flatworms slither across the forest floor after it has rained. Can you find four?

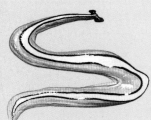

Weevils often have long noses, but giraffe-necked weevils have long necks. Find four.

Huge emperor dragonflies catch insects flying past. Can you spot six of them?

Some stick insects grow fake "moss" on their bodies as a disguise. Find three.

Thorn spiders look like prickly jewels in their huge webs. Find four.

Giant millipedes can be poisonous, so few animals eat them. Can you find five?

This praying mantis nymph is very well disguised. Can you spot four?

Green lynx spiders blend in with their leafy surroundings. Find four.

Pill millipedes can't run from enemies. They roll into a ball instead. Spot six.

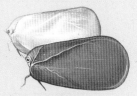

Rosea bugs look a little like leaves. If a bird pecks one, the whole group flies off. Find 27.

Hairy weevils only live in Madagascar. Spot seven of each of these.

Longhorn beetles lay their eggs in dead wood. Later, their larvae eat it. Find seven.

Hissing cockroaches hiss by blowing air out of two holes in their tummies. Find five.

Can you find four shield bug adults and four nymphs?

Adult

Nymph

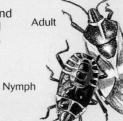

Spot six butterflies with their wings open and five with their wings shut.

201

Dazzling display

Some of the most beautiful insects in the world live in rainforests, but they are often hard to spot. Can you find 95 minibeasts in this rainforest in Peru, in South America?

A wandering spider's bite is so poisonous it can kill a person. Can you find two?

Thornbugs look like thorns. Their disguise fools hungry birds. Spot ten.

When Hamadryas butterflies fly, their wings make clicking noises. Can you spot four?

Find nine leaf beetles.

Some assassin bugs have spiky bodies. Enemies find them hard to chew. Can you find seven?

Hawk moth caterpillars look pretty but taste nasty, so birds leave them alone. Spot five.

Many gorgeous grasshoppers live in these forests. Find three of each of these kinds.

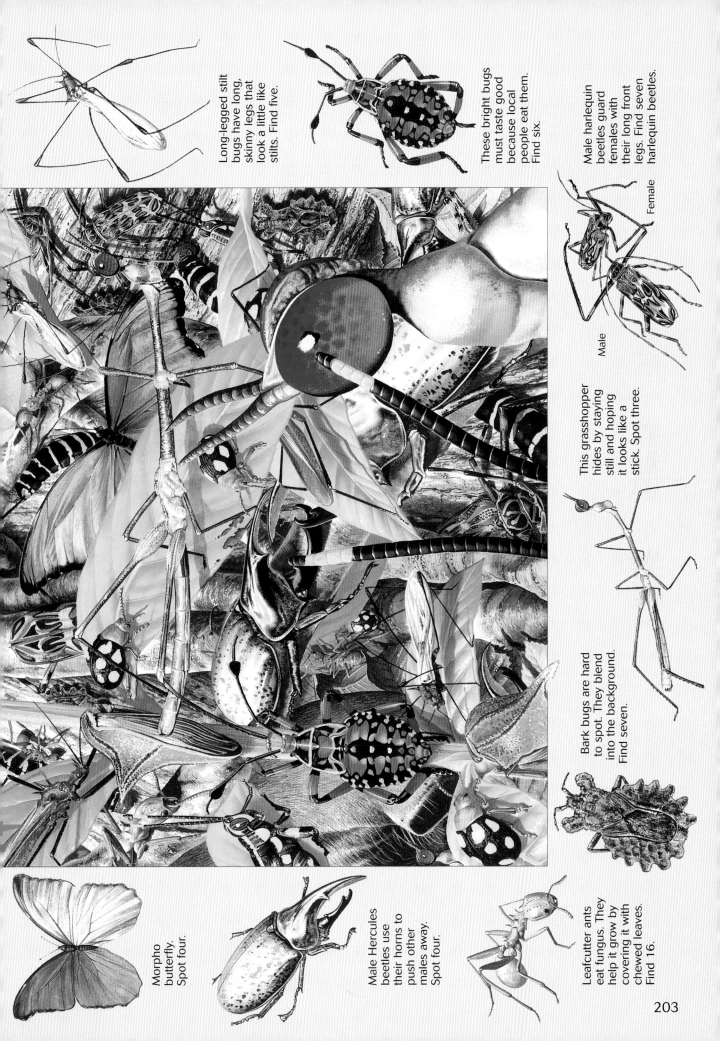

Long-legged stilt bugs have long, skinny legs that look a little like stilts. Find five.

These bright bugs must taste good because local people eat them. Find six.

Male harlequin beetles guard females with their long front legs. Find seven harlequin beetles.

Female

Male

This grasshopper hides by staying still and hoping it looks like a stick. Spot three.

Bark bugs are hard to spot. They blend into the background. Find seven.

Morpho butterfly. Spot four.

Male Hercules beetles use their horns to push other males away. Spot four.

Leafcutter ants eat fungus. They help it grow by covering it with chewed leaves. Find 16.

203

Between the trees

All kinds of amazing bugs live in the thick eucalyptus forests of eastern Australia. Ants as big as your toes go marching past, and poisonous spiders lurk in dark corners.

Emperor gum moths only lay their eggs on eucalyptus trees. Find three.

Sawfly larvae wave their heads and spit bitter liquid at their enemies. Find nine.

Female redback spiders are much more poisonous than males. Can you spot three?

Processionary moth caterpillars leave a long silk thread behind them. Find 11.

Fierce Sydney funnel-web spiders only live near the city of Sydney. Spot four.

Bulldog ants are the biggest, fiercest ants in the world. Can you spot 12 of them?

Giant stick insects unfold their wings to give enemies a shock. Can you find four?

Net throwing spiders throw a net of silk over their victims. Spot two more.

Some crickets flash their bright backs at enemies to scare them. Find five.

Bogong moths can eat whole fields of grain if they get together. Spot four.

Common grass yellow butterflies sip water from puddles in hot weather. Spot 23.

Emperor gum moth caterpillars have bright spikes to warn enemies off. Find four.

Gliding spiders can stretch out two flaps of skin and glide through the air. Find four.

Some people dig moth caterpillars called "witchetty grubs" out of tree trunks and eat them. Find six.

There are over 450 different types of shield bugs in Australia. Can you spot nine of this kind?

Monarch butterflies can fly up to 130km (80 miles) in one day. Find five.

Water world

Ponds are perfect homes for many small creatures. They are often nurseries for young insects too. Can you spot 121 minibeasts in this North American pond?

Fisher spiders crawl down plants, catch fish, then haul them up to eat. Spot eight.

Tube

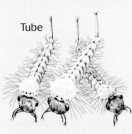

Mosquito larvae dangle under the surface of ponds. They breathe through a tube. Spot seven.

Backswimmers swim upside down, using their back legs as oars. Find six.

Stoneflies can't fly well, so they sit beside the water most of the time. Spot nine.

Damselflies can't walk well. They use their legs to grab hold of plants. Spot seven.

Water striders skim lightly across the surface of the pond. Spot eight water striders.

Fishermen put fake caddisflies on their hooks to attract fish. Spot six real caddisflies.

Pond snails do a very useful job. They eat plants and make the water much clearer. Find 11.

Great diving beetle larvae bite their victims and then suck out their insides. Find five.

Water scorpions lurk just below the surface, grabbing passing insects. Spot six.

Dragonfly nymphs have jaws that shoot out to crunch up food. Can you spot five?

Caddisfly larvae are safe inside a case covered with pebbles and shells. Find five.

Whirligig beetles can look into the air and under the water at the same time. Find 15.

Great diving beetles have strong back legs to help them swim and dive. Spot ten.

Water stick insects breathe air through a narrow breathing tube. Find five stick insects.

Adult mayflies never eat. They just mate, lay eggs and die. Find nine.

207

In the woods

If you walked through this wood in northern France, thousands of eyes might be watching you. Tiny creatures make their homes up in the trees, or down on the ground.

Male stag beetles fight with their sharp antlers, but rarely hurt each other. Find six.

Wood ants squirt acid out of their bottoms to attack enemies. Can you spot 20?

Crane flies have six legs. They can survive losing one or two of them. Find eight.

Hedge snails are easy for birds to spot, so they try to stay hidden. Find six snails.

Darter dragonflies flit through the trees in woodland clearings. Can you spot three?

Male empid flies give females a bug wrapped in silk while they mate. Find 12.

Bumblebees fly from flower to flower, collecting pollen. Spot four bumblebees.

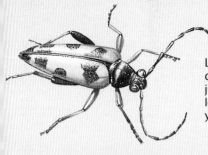

Antenna

Longhorn beetles don't have horns, just antennae that look like them. Can you spot seven?

Burying beetles lay their eggs next to a dead animal. When the eggs hatch into larvae, they eat it. Spot ten.

Hornets chew bark to make a soggy mixture. They use it to build nests. Find four.

The amount of purple you can see on a purple emperor butterfly's wings depends on the light. Spot six.

Bark beetles lay their eggs in tree bark. When the eggs hatch, the larvae eat the bark. Find 11.

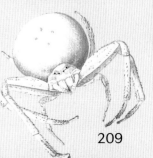

Large black slugs slither along the woodland floor, leaving a slimy trail. Spot seven.

Poplar hawk moths can see in the dark, so they fly at night. Find five.

Male horseflies drink plant juices but females need to drink animals' blood. Spot four.

Crab spiders lie in wait for insects in flowers. Then they attack and kill them. Spot three.

209

Swamp life

Lots of bugs live together in the dark, murky water of the Everglades swamp in Florida.

There are pools of fresh water and patches of salt water, with different bugs in each.

Golden orb weaver spiders spin huge webs above the water. Spot three.

Eggs

Apple snails climb out of the water to lay eggs. Find six snails and three clumps of eggs.

Io moths have markings like eyes on their wings. They flash them at enemies. Spot five.

Male fiddler crabs wave their big front claw to look fierce. Find five more.

Huge swarms of mosquitoes live here. They can give people painful bites. Spot 14.

Jumping spider. Spot three.

Tree snails' shells can have over 40 patterns. Can you spot two of each of these?

Viceroy butterflies drink sweet liquid called nectar from plants. Can you see five?

Blue land crabs scuttle along the mangrove tree roots. Can you find 14?

Green darner dragonflies swoop over the water, looking for insects to eat. Find five.

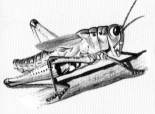

A lubber grasshopper's thick skin protects it from enemies' teeth. Find four.

Fisher spiders always find plenty to eat in the Everglades. Can you find three?

Female giant water bugs stick eggs onto males' backs. Spot three males and a female.

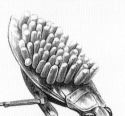

Midge larvae float in the water, eating tiny bugs. Spot seven midge larvae.

Zebra butterflies lay their eggs on passionflower leaves. Can you see four?

211

Deep in the jungle

The jungles of southeast Asia are as busy by night as they are by day. The left-hand page shows who comes out in the daytime and the right-hand page shows the night.

Hairy bird-eating spiders really do eat birds. They can climb trees too. Find four.

Fireflies' tummies light up, then flash on and off. Find 11.

Cockchafer beetle. Find seven.

Stay away from red centipedes. Their bites are very painful. Can you spot five?

Atlas moths are the largest moths in the world. Look hard and try to find three.

Snails slither around the jungle. Find three of each of these two kinds of snails.

Longicorn beetles use their long feelers to explore the jungle. Can you see five?

Loepa moths have no tongues. They don't live long enough to need food. Find four.

Lantern bugs got their name because they often flutter around people's lanterns. Spot ten.

Flat-backed millipedes eat fungi that grows on trees. Can you find five of them?

These shield bugs taste horrible, so other animals don't eat them. Find seven.

Brilliant jewel beetles like lying on leaves in the warm sunshine. Find eight.

Termites march to and fro on the jungle floor. Can you spot 16 termites here?

Male cicadas make a chirping sound with a part of their tummies. Find five.

Birdwing butterflies are as big as a hand when their wings are open. Spot four.

Weaver ants make nests by sticking leaves together with spit. Can you spot 12?

Nephila spiders spin webs out of pale yellow silk. Can you spot four of them?

Minibeast safari

People go on expeditions, or safaris, to see the wildlife of Africa. They may not see the thousands of bugs that live there too. Spot 118 in this picture of part of South Africa.

Male rhinoceros beetles have a horn like a rhinoceros. Can you see five?

Tsetse flies drink other creatures' blood through a tube-shaped mouth. Find ten.

Swallowtail butterfly

Swallowtail caterpillar

These caterpillars wave smelly horns at enemies. Can you spot five caterpillars and three butterflies?

Potter wasps put caterpillars in their nests as food for their larvae. Find five potter wasps.

African land snails are the largest snails in the world. Can you spot four of them?

African assassin bugs work as a team, killing other insects. Find five.

Longhorn beetles chew their way into tree trunks. Find seven longhorn beetles.

African moon moths flash the eye-like markings on their wings at enemies. Spot three.

Hanging flies hang upside down from twigs with their long, skinny legs. Find eight.

Monarch butterflies eat plants that make their flesh taste horrible. Find four.

Histerid beetles like eating dung, or the bodies of dead animals. Find 21.

Ground beetles can squirt burning acid out of their bottoms. Can you spot four?

Processionary moth. Find three.

Processionary moth caterpillars wriggle along the ground in a long line. Spot ten.

Stalk-eyed flies got their name from their eyes. It's easy to see why. Find four.

A swarm of hungry locusts can eat a whole crop in hours. Spot 11 locusts.

If you disturb a praying mantis, it might wave its back wings at you. Spot six.

215

Insect city

Termites live in huge family groups. They build a mound of mud, spit and dung, and make a nest inside. This is what the nest looks like.

Termite mound

Only the queen termite lays eggs. She can lay over 30,000 a day. Can you find her?

All the king termite does is mate with the queen. Can you spot him?

Worker

Eggs

Worker termites take eggs to parts of the nest called nurseries. Find four nurseries.

Worker

Larvae

The eggs hatch into pale larvae. Worker termites care for them. Find 23 larvae.

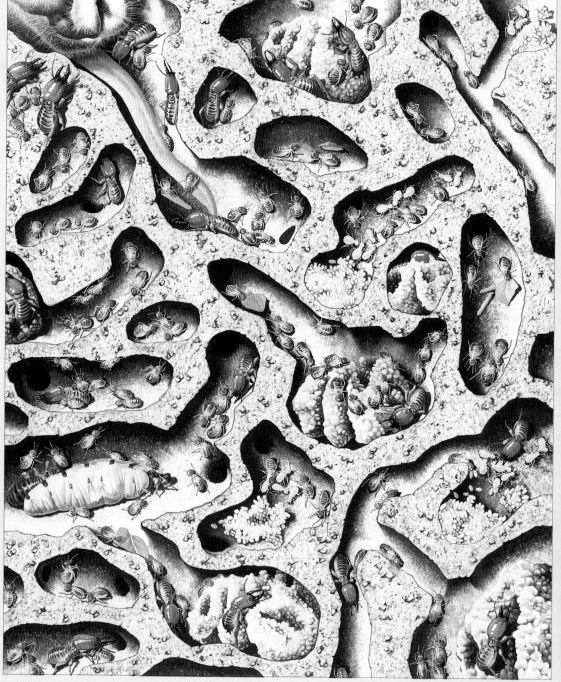

Soldier termites keep guard. They bite enemies, or squirt liquid at them. Spot 20.

Workers carry leaves into the nest in their mouths. Spot seven doing this job.

Fungus grows in "fungus gardens" in the nest. The termites eat it. Find six gardens.

Busy beehive

People keep honeybees in hives. The bees collect nectar and pollen from flowers. They eat the pollen and make the nectar into honey.

Beehive

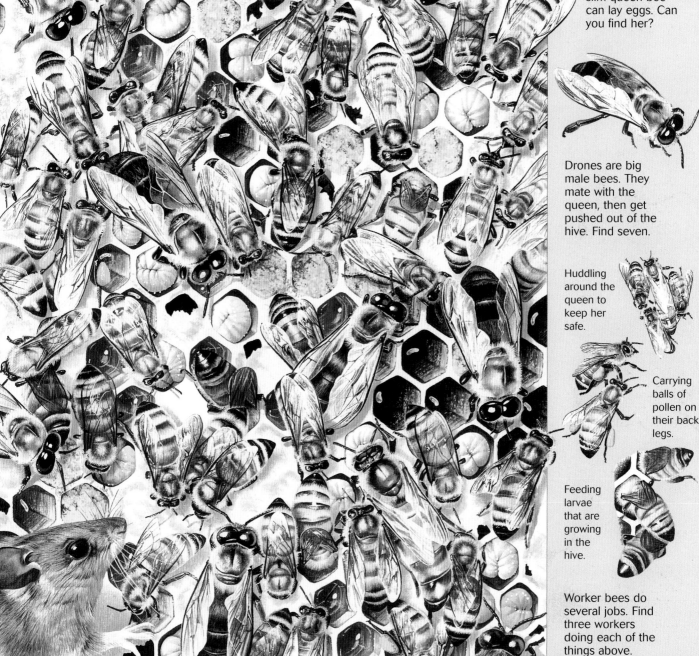

Only the long, slim queen bee can lay eggs. Can you find her?

Drones are big male bees. They mate with the queen, then get pushed out of the hive. Find seven.

Huddling around the queen to keep her safe.

Carrying balls of pollen on their back legs.

Feeding larvae that are growing in the hive.

Worker bees do several jobs. Find three workers doing each of the things above.

Bees build little wax boxes called cells in the hive. Spot the cells being used for these things.

Find 17 cells with larvae in them.

Find ten cells full of pollen.

Worker bees sometimes spit food into another bee's mouth. Find one doing this.

Find 14 cells full of honey.

Find 12 cells with bee eggs in them.

217

Around the world

This map of the world shows the places where all the bugs in this book live.

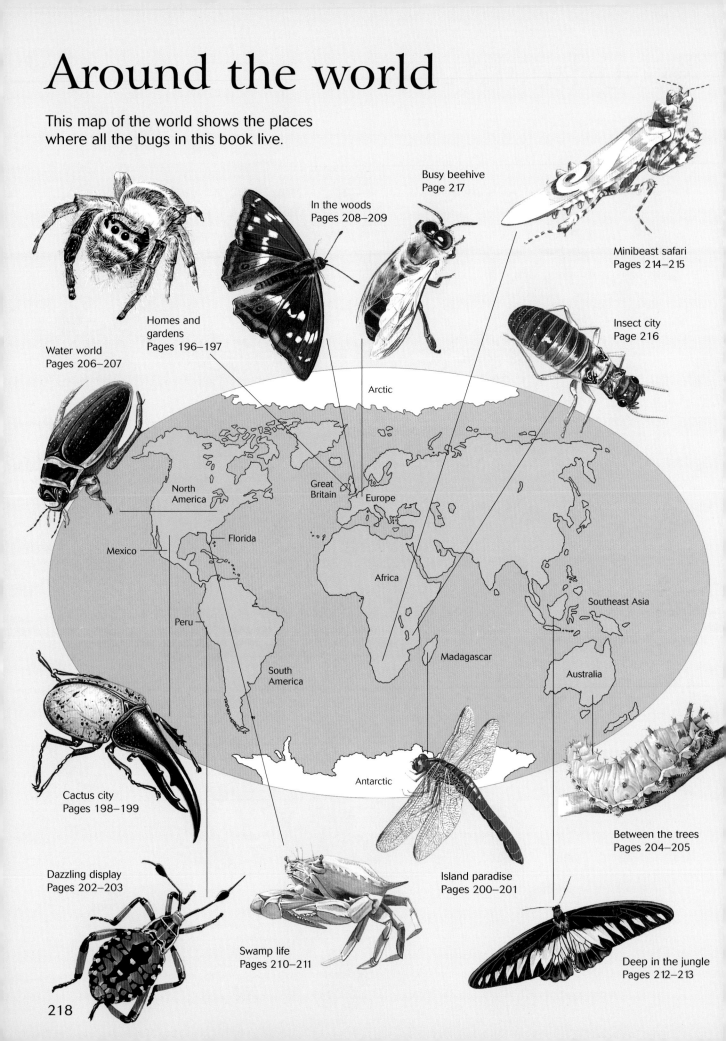

Busy beehive
Page 217

Minibeast safari
Pages 214–215

In the woods
Pages 208–209

Insect city
Page 216

Homes and
gardens
Pages 196–197

Water world
Pages 206–207

Arctic

North
America

Great
Britain

Europe

Mexico

Florida

Africa

Southeast Asia

Peru

South
America

Madagascar

Australia

Antarctic

Cactus city
Pages 198–199

Between the trees
Pages 204–205

Dazzling display
Pages 202–203

Island paradise
Pages 200–201

Swamp life
Pages 210–211

Deep in the jungle
Pages 212–213

Big bug puzzle

You've seen all these bugs earlier in this part of the book, but can you remember anything about them?

To do this puzzle, you may need to look back and find which page they're on. The answers are on page 223.

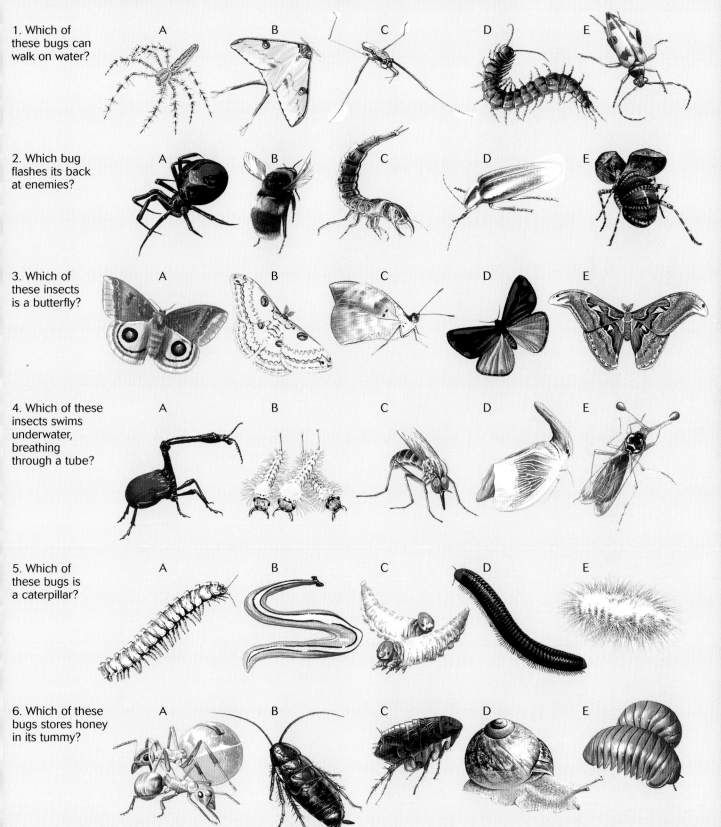

1. Which of these bugs can walk on water?

A B C D E

2. Which bug flashes its back at enemies?

A B C D E

3. Which of these insects is a butterfly?

A B C D E

4. Which of these insects swims underwater, breathing through a tube?

A B C D E

5. Which of these bugs is a caterpillar?

A B C D E

6. Which of these bugs stores honey in its tummy?

A B C D E

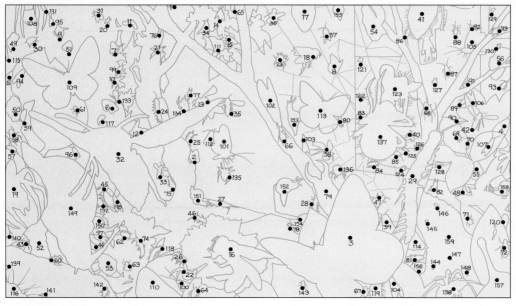

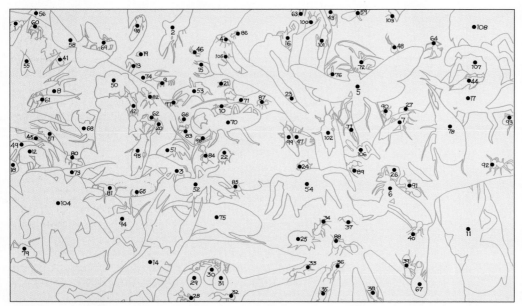

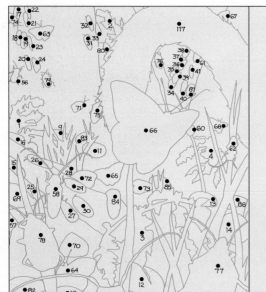

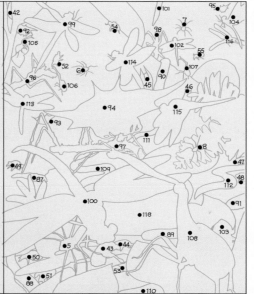

Homes and gardens 196–197

Male common blue butterflies 1 2 3 4
Female common blue butterflies 5 6 7 8
Honeybees 9 10 11 12 13 14 15 16 17 18
Zebra spiders 19 20 21 22 23
Centipedes 24 25 26 27 28 29
Wasps 30 31 32 33 34 35 36 37 38 39 40 41 42
Devil's coach-horses 43 44 45 46 47 48
Spittle bugs 49 50 51 52 53 54 55 56
Greenflies 57 58 59 60 61 62 63 64 65 66 67 68 69 70 71 72 73
Earwigs 74 75 76 77 78 79 80 81 82

Cockroaches 83 84 85 86 87 88 89 90 91 92 93
Lacewings 94 95 96 97 98 99 100 101 102 103 104 105 106 107
Cinnabar moths 108 109 110 111 112 113 114
Cinnabar moth caterpillars 115 116 117 118 119 120
Houseflies 121 122 123 124 125 126 127 128 129 130
Garden spiders 131 132 133 134 135 136 137 138
Fleas 139 140 141 142 143 144 145 146 147 148
Snails 149 150 151 152 153 154 155 156 157 158
Cat 159

Cactus city 198–199

Tarantula hawk wasps 1 2 3 4 5 6 7
Trapdoor spiders 8 9 10 11
Scorpions 12 13 14 15 16 17
Giant red velvet mites 18 19 20 21 22 23 24 25 26 27
Honey ants 28 29 30 31 32 33 34 35 36 37 38 39 40
Blister beetles 41 42 43 44
Black widow spiders 45 46 47 48
Tarantulas 49 50 51 52 53 54
Yucca moths 55 56 57 58 59
Lynx spiders 60 61 62 63 64

Ant-lion larvae 65 66 67
Whip scorpions 68 69 70 71 72
Hercules beetles 73 74 75 76 77 78
Harvester ants 79 80 81 82 83 84 85 86 87 88 89 90 91 92 93
Painted grasshoppers 94 95 96 97 98 99 100 101 102 103
Red-kneed bird-eating spiders 104 105 106 107
Burrowing owl 108

Island paradise 200–201

Praying mantis nymphs 1 2 3 4
Lynx spiders 5 6 7 8
Pill millipedes 9 10 11 12 13 14
Rosea bugs 15 16 17 18 19 20 21 22 23 24 25 26 27 28 29 30 31 32 33 34 35 36 37 38 39 40 41
Yellow hairy weevils 42 43 44 45 46 47 48
Brown hairy weevils 49 50 51 52 53 54 55
Longhorn beetles 56 57 58 59 60 61 62
Butterflies with open wings 63 64 65 66 67 68
Butterflies with shut wings 69 70 71 72 73

Shield bug adults 74 75 76 77
Shield bug nymphs 78 79 80 81
Hissing cockroaches 82 83 84 85 86
Giant millipedes 87 88 89 90 91
Thorn spiders 92 93 94 95
Stick insects 96 97 98
Emperor dragonflies 99 100 101 102 103 104
Giraffe-necked weevils 105 106 107 108
Flatworms 109 110 111 112
Red dragonflies 113 114 115 116
Ring-tailed lemur 117
Blue tree boa 118

220

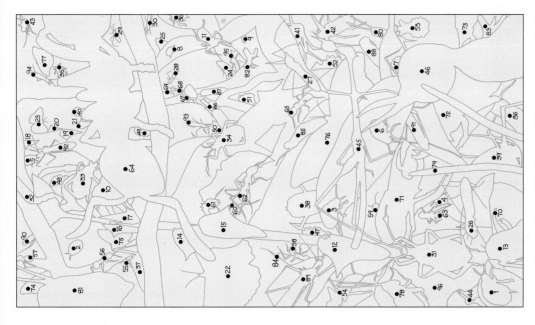

Dazzling display 202–203

Leaf beetles 1 3 4
5 6 7 8 9

Wandering spiders
10 11

Thornbugs 12 13
14 15 16 17 18
19 20 21

Hamadryas
butterflies 22 23 24
25

Stilt bugs 26 27 28
29 30

Bright bugs 31 32
33 34 35 36

Harlequin beetles
37 38 39 40 41
42 43

Grasshoppers 44
45 46

Bark bugs 47 48 49
50 51 52 53

Leafcutter ants 54
55 56 57 58 59
60 61 62 63 64
65 66 67 68 69

Hercules beetles 70
71 72 73

Morpho butterflies
74 75 76 77

Black and yellow
grasshoppers 78 79
80

Yellow, black and
red grasshoppers
81 82 83

Hawk moth
caterpillars 84 85
86 87 88

Assassin bugs 89
90 91 92 93 94
95

Tapir 96

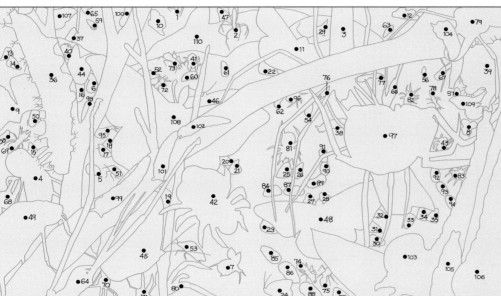

Between the trees 204–205

Net throwing spiders
1 2 3

Crickets 4 5 6 7 8

Bogong moths 9 10
11 12

Common grass
yellow butterflies 13
14 15 16 17 18
19 20 21 22 23
24 25 26 27 28
29 30 31 32 33
34 35

Emperor gum moth
caterpillars 36 37
38 39

Gliding spiders 40
41 42 43

Monarch butterflies
44 45 46 47 48

Shield bugs 49 50
51 52 53 54 55
56 57

Witchetty grubs 58
59 60 61 62 63

Giant stick insects
64 65 66 67

Bulldog ants 68 69
70 71 72 73 74
75 76 77 78 79

Sydney funnel-web
spiders 80 81
82 83

Processionary moth
caterpillars 84 85
86 87 88 89 90
91 92 93 94

Redback spiders 95
96 97

Sawfly larvae 98
99 100 101 102
103 104 105
106

Emperor gum moths
107 108 109

Bandicoot 110

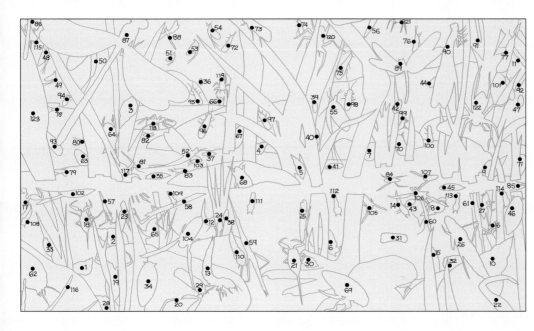

Water world 206–207

Pond snails 1 2 3 4
5 6 7 8 9 10 11

Great diving beetle
larvae 12 13 14 15
16

Water scorpions 17
18 19 20 21 22

Dragonfly nymphs
23 24 25 26 27

Caddisfly larvae 28
29 30 31 32

Whirligig beetles
33 34 35 36 37
38 39 40 41 42
43 44 45 46 47

Mayflies 48 49 50
51 52 53 54 55
56

Water stick insects
57 58 59 60 61

Great diving beetles
62 63 64 65 66
67 68 69 70 71

Caddisflies 72 73
74 75 76 77

Water striders 78 79
80 81 82 83 84
85

Damselflies 86 87
88 89 90 91 92

Stoneflies 93 94 95
96 97 98 99 100
101

Backswimmers 102
103 104 105
106 107

Mosquito larvae
108 109 110 111
112 113 114

Fisher spiders 115
116 117 118 119
120 121 122

Great white heron
123

221

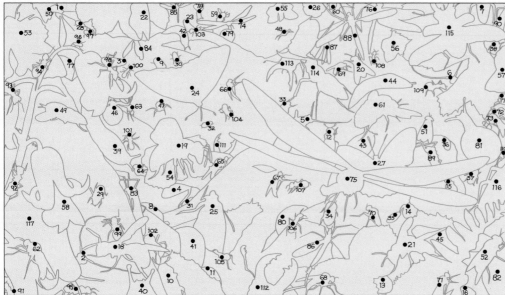

In the woods 208–209

Longhorn beetles 1
2 3 4 5 6 7
Burying beetles 8 9
10 11 12 13 14 15
16 17
Hornets 18 19 20
21
Purple emperor
butterflies 22 23 24
25 26 27
Bark beetles 28 29
30 31 32 33 34
35 36 37 38
Slugs 39 40 41 42
43 44 45
Crab spiders 46 47
48
Horseflies 49 50 51
52
Poplar hawk moths
53 54 55 56 57
Bumblebees 58 59
60 61
Empid flies 62 63
64 65 66 67 68
69 70 71 72 73
Darter dragonflies
74 75 76

Hedge snails 77 78
79 80 81 82
Crane flies 83 84 85
86 87 88 89 90
Wood ants 91 92 93
94 95 96 97 98
99 100 101 102
103 104 105 106
107 108 109 110
Stag beetles 111 112
113 114 115 116
Hedgehog 117

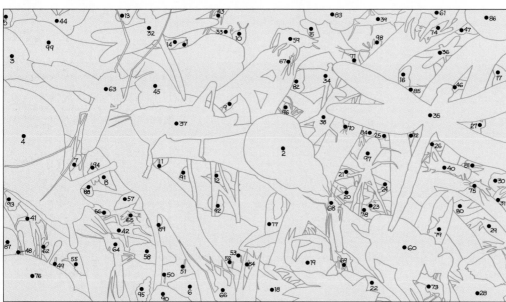

Swamp life 210–211

Tree snails 1 2 3 4
5 6 7 8 9 10 11
12
Viceroy butterflies 13
14 15 16 17
Blue land crabs 18
19 20 21 22 23
24 25 26 27 28
29 30 31
Green darner
dragonflies 32 33
34 35 36
Lubber grasshoppers
37 38 39 40
Fisher spiders 41 42
43
Zebra butterflies 44
45 46 47
Midge larvae 48 49
50 51 52 53 54
Giant water bugs 55
56 57 58
Jumping spiders 59
60 61
Mosquitoes 62 63
64 65 66 67 68
69 70 71 72 73
74 75

Fiddler crabs 76 77
78 79 80 81
Io moths 82 83 84
85 86
Apple snails 87 88
89 90 91 92
Apple snail eggs 93
94 95
Golden orb weaver
spiders 96 97 98
Alligator 99

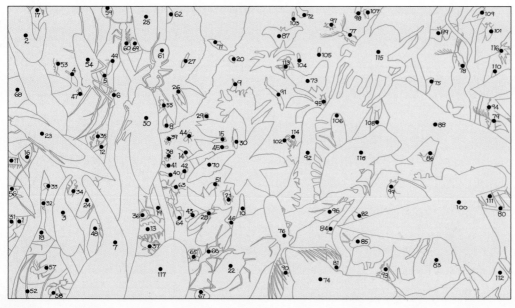

Deep in the jungle 212–213

Lantern bugs 1 2 3
4 5 6 7 8 9
10 Flat-backed
millipedes 11 12 13
14 15
Shield bugs 16 17
18 19 20 21 22
Jewel beetles 23 24
25 26 27 28 29
30
Termites 31 32 33
34 35 36 37 38
39 40 41 42 43
44 45 46
Cicadas 47 48 49
50 51
Nephila spiders 52
53 54 55
Weaver ants 56 57
58 59 60 61 62
63 64 65 66 67
Birdwing butterflies
68 69 70 71
Loepa moths 72 73
74 75
Longicorn beetles
76 77 78 79 80

Yellow snails 81 82
83
Brown snails 84 85
86
Atlas moths 87 88
89
Red centipedes 90
91 92 93 94
Cockchafer beetles
95 96 97 98 99
100 101
Fireflies 102 103
104 105 106 107
108 109 110 111
112
Hairy bird-eating
spiders 113 114 115
116
Orang-utan 117
Green tree frog 118

222

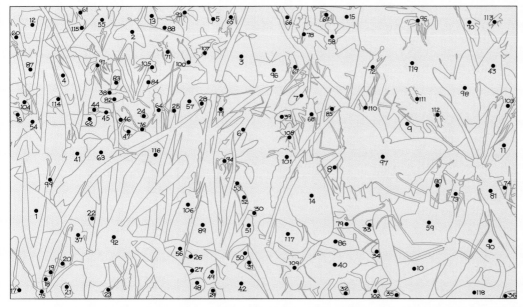

Minibeast safari 214–215

African moon moths
1 2 3
Hanging flies 4 5 6
7 8 9 10 11
Monarch butterflies
12 13 14 15
Histerid beetles 16
17 18 19 20 21
22 23 24 25 26
27 28 29 30 31
32 33 34 35 36
Ground beetles 37
38 39 40
Processionary moths
41 42 43
Processionary moth
caterpillars 44 45
46 47 48 49 50
51 52 53
Praying mantids 54
55 56 57 58 59
Locusts 60 61 62
63 64 65 66 67
68 69 70
Stalk-eyed flies 71
72 73 74
Longhorn beetles 75
76 77 78 79 80
81

African assassin bugs
82 83 84 85
86
African land snails
87 88 89 90
Potter wasps 91 92
93 94 95
Swallowtail butterflies
96 97 98
Swallowtail butterfly
caterpillars 99 100
101 102 103
Tsetse flies 104 105
106 107 108 109
110 111 112 113
Rhinoceros beetles
114 115 116 117
118
Kudu 119

Insect city 216

Fungus gardens 72
73 74 75 76 77
Workers carrying
leaves 78 79 80 81
82 83 84
Soldier termites 85
86 87 88 89 90
91 92 93 94 95
96 97 98 99 100
101 102 103 104

Larvae 105 106
107 108 109 110
111 112 113 114 115
116 117 118 119
120 121 122 123
124 125 126 127
Nurseries 128 129
130 131
King termite 132
Queen termite 133
Aardvark 134

Busy beehive 217

Queen bee 1
Drones 2 3 4 5 6 7
8
Workers huddling
around the queen 9
10 11
Workers carrying
balls of pollen 12 13
14
Workers feeding
larvae 15 16 17
Worker spitting 18
Pollen cells 19 20
21 22 23 24 25
26 27 28

Egg cells 29 30 31
32 33 34 35 36
37 38 39 40
Larvae cells 41 42
43 44 45 46 47
48 49 50 51 52
53 54 55 56 57
Honey cells 58 59
60 61 62 63 64
65 66 67 68 69
70 71
Mouse 135

Answers to the Big bug puzzle on page 219: 1C 2E 3C 4B 5E 6A

Part Seven

PLANET EARTH
SEARCH

Part Seven

Planet Earth Search

This part of the book is filled with pictures of all kinds of places around the world, from deserts to rainforests. There are lots of things for you to spot in each picture. Can you find them all? If you get stuck, the answers are on pages 252–255. The example below shows you how each puzzle works.

A red square on the globe in the corner of the page shows you where in the world the scene is set.

Each little picture shows you what to look for in the big picture.

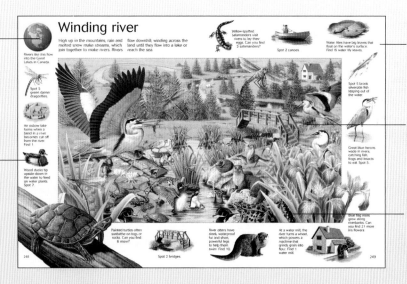

The writing next to each little picture tells you how many of that thing you need to find.

You will have to look hard to spot these iris flowers in the distance.

This salamander is partly hidden, but don't miss it out.

To make the puzzles more fun, each big picture shows lots of things to spot very close together. In real life, these places are much less crowded.

About Planet Earth

Earth is one of eight planets that travel around, or orbit, the Sun. It has many amazing features, from snow-capped mountains to dark, underground caves. It is the only planet where we know that plants and animals live.

World climates

Earth is a place of extremes. It can be freezing cold in the Arctic and extremely hot at the Equator. Which kinds of plants and animals live in an area depends on the weather the area usually has, known as its climate. In this part of the book, you can explore places with many different climates. If you look back at this map, you can find out where else in the world has a similar climate.

Climate key

This shows which different climates the shading on the map represents:

Mountains – cold for much of the year

Polar climate – very cold all year

Temperate climate – some rain in all seasons

Warm climate – summers are hot and dry, winters are mild and wet

Desert climate – hot and very dry all year

Tropical climate – hot all year, with heavy rain in the wet season

Equatorial climate – hot and wet, with heavy rain

pages 236–237

NORTH AMERICA

pages 240–241

pages 248–249

pages 238–239

Atlantic Ocean

pages 242–243

SOUTH AMERICA

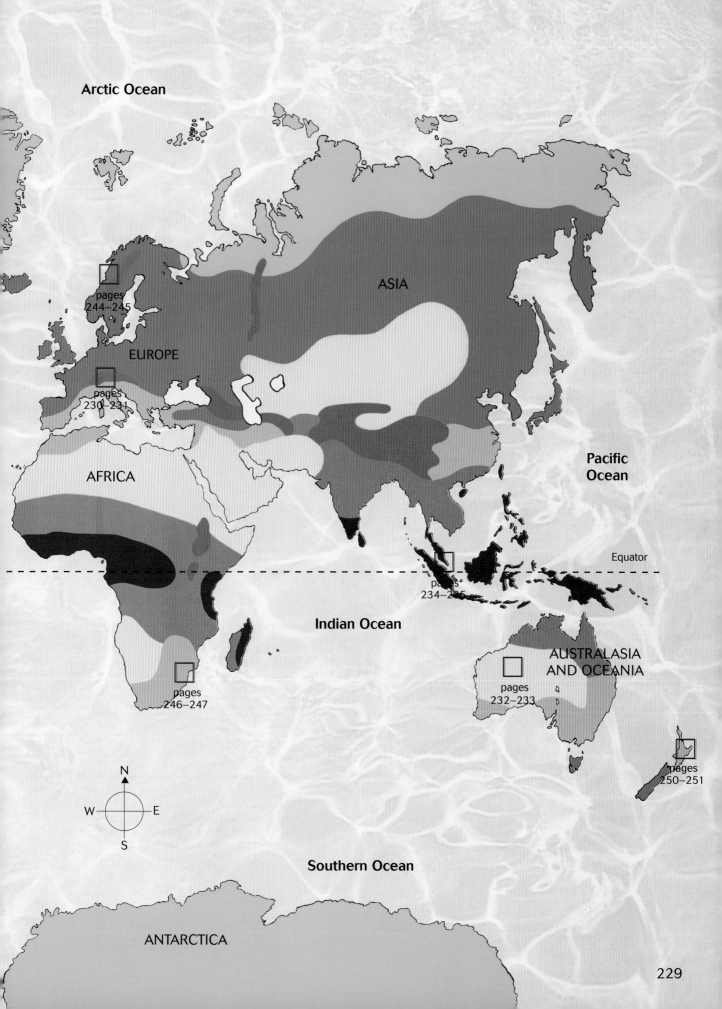

Arctic Ocean

ASIA

EUROPE

pages
244–245

pages
230–231

AFRICA

Pacific
Ocean

Equator

pages
234–235

Indian Ocean

AUSTRALASIA
AND OCEANIA

pages
232–233

pages
246–247

pages
250–251

N

W   E

S

Southern Ocean

ANTARCTICA

Alpine slopes

It's much colder and windier on the higher Alpine slopes than in the valleys below. Many mountain animals have thick fur to keep them warm. Even plants have adapted to living in a cold climate.

The Alps are the highest mountains in Europe.

Many mountain peaks are covered in snow all year round. Find six snowy peaks.

Wallcreepers search for small insects to eat. Spot three wallcreepers.

Edelweiss plants have furry leaves to protect them from the cold. Find ten edelweiss flowers.

Alpine hares have brown fur in summer and white fur in winter. This makes them hard for predators to spot all year round. Spot 12 more Alpine hares.

A glacier is a river of ice that slides slowly downhill. Can you find two glaciers?

230

Mountain houses, or chalets, have steep roofs and overhanging eaves. Spot 16 chalets.

Spot eight purple-shot copper butterflies.

Cable cars carry people up and down the slopes. Find five.

Golden eagles circle in the air, looking for hares to eat. Spot three golden eagles.

Can you see six hot-air balloons?

Cumulus clouds have flat bottoms and puffy tops. Find nine.

Alpine ibexes climb about on rocky mountain slopes to graze. Spot 18.

Gliders don't have engines. They use the wind to help them fly. Find two.

Spruce trees grow low down on the slopes. Higher up, it is too cold and windy for them. Spot 15.

Australia

Australian desert

Deserts are the driest places on Earth. Most are baking hot during the day and freezing cold at night.

Few animals and plants live in deserts because there is little water or shelter for them.

Deserts cover most of central Australia.

Tumbleweed plants scatter seeds as they are blown along by the wind. Spot nine.

Baobab trees store water in their swollen, barrel-like trunks. Can you find five more?

A dust devil is a moving spiral of air and dust. Spot one.

Kangaroos can't walk. They hop everywhere, using their tails to balance. Find six.

A mesa is an isolated hill with steep sides and a flat top. Can you spot four mesas?

Bushfires often start when lightning strikes plants or trees. Find one bushfire.

An oasis is a fertile area of a desert, where water is found. Spot two oases.

Emus are large flightless birds. Find five.

Woma pythons hunt for lizards, birds and small animals to eat. Spot four.

Spot five tents.

Lightning is a bolt of electricity in the sky. Find two bolts of lightning.

Thorny devils look fierce, but really they're harmless. Their spikes protect them from attackers. Spot three more thorny devils.

The Aboriginal people of Australia make hand prints on rocks that are sacred to them. Spot five more hand prints.

Asia

Mangrove swamp

Mangroves are trees that grow along tropical shores where rivers meet the sea. The water is a mix of fresh water from the river and salt water from the sea. Mangroves have adapted to grow in salty water.

Mangrove swamps are found along the coasts of southeast Asia.

Mangrove seedlings drop into the water and float until they reach mud banks, where they take root. Find 29.

Male fiddler crabs have one claw bigger than the other. They use their big claws to fight over females. Spot six males.

Hawksbill turtles use their sharp, beaky mouths to break open shellfish. Spot two more.

Mudskippers are fish that can breathe both in and out of water. They use their fins to climb onto mangrove roots. Find nine.

Spot seven oysters.

Saltwater crocodiles sometimes leap out of the water to catch birds. Spot two crocodiles.

Mangrove trees have unusual, stilt-like roots, which stop their trunks from toppling over in the mud. Find five more mangrove trees.

Little egrets roost in mangroves. When the tide is out, they wade in the shallow water and catch fish. Spot three little egrets.

Cownose rays usually swim near the surface, but sink to the bottom to hunt for clams. Can you spot ten?

Fishermen build huts on stilts in the sea. They tie their fishing nets to the stilts. Can you find one hut?

People use kayaks to explore the mangroves without disturbing the wildlife. Find three kayaks.

Silver moony fish hide from danger among the mangrove roots. Spot 15 more moony fish.

Banded sea kraits swim underwater, but come to the surface to breathe. Spot six.

Icy Arctic

Greenland is a large island in the Arctic Ocean.

The temperature in Greenland is usually well below freezing, and in winter the surface of the sea freezes over, forming a layer of sea ice. In this picture, it is spring and most of the sea ice has melted.

People use snowmobiles to explore the icy landscape. Spot two snowmobiles.

Lemmings use their claws like shovels to burrow into the snow. Spot three lemmings.

Some people travel around on sleds pulled by husky dogs. Find one sled pulled by dogs.

Spot 12 walruses.

Most goods are flown into villages, because Greenland doesn't have many roads. Spot one cargo plane.

Polar bears have very thick fur to keep them warm. Can you see two more adults and two cubs?

Unlike other owls, snowy owls hunt during the day. They catch small birds and lemmings. Find three more snowy owls.

Male narwhals have a long, pointed tusk. Spot two narwhals.

Arctic foxes hunt lemmings. They pound the snow with their paws to break into their burrows. Find three Arctic foxes.

Musk oxen have long, woolly fur that hangs almost to their feet. Spot six.

An iceberg is a chunk of ice floating in the sea. You can only see one seventh of an iceberg above water. Spot seven icebergs.

Most Greenlanders live along the coast, in small villages of brightly painted wooden houses. Spot 11 wooden houses.

Caribou eat plants called lichens in winter. They sniff them out under the snow. Can you find 12 more caribou?

Limestone caves like this are found in Missouri, USA.

Ferns need sunlight to make their food, so they only grow where light shines. Find five.

A sink-hole is a hole in the roof of a cave, which lets sunlight in. Spot three sink-holes.

Snakes sometimes fall through sink-holes into caves. Spot four rat snakes.

Find ten cave crickets.

Limestone cave

Limestone is a type of rock that wears away easily. When rain seeps into cracks in limestone, the cracks slowly widen. Over thousands of years, large underground caves can form.

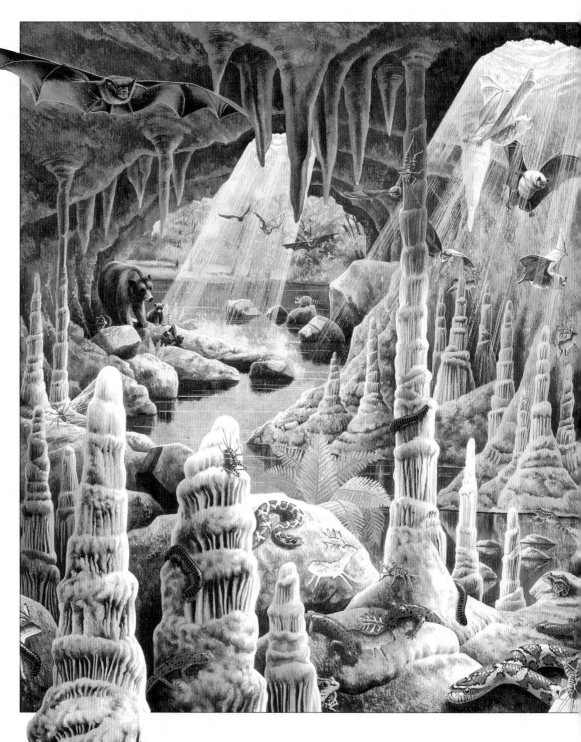

As water splashes onto the cave floor, it deposits minerals, which slowly build up into cone shapes called stalagmites. Spot 32 more stalagmites.

Giant millipedes often shelter in caves. Find nine giant millipedes.

As water drips through the cave roof, it leaves behind minerals. Over time, the minerals build up into icicle shapes called stalactites. Spot 29 stalactites.

Little brown bats fly into caves to sleep during the day. Spot 30 more.

Early humans carved pictures of the animals they hunted in rock. Can you see eight deer pictures?

When a stalactite meets a stalagmite, they join to form a column. Find four columns.

Fossils are the remains of dead animals and plants that have slowly turned to rock. Spot five crinoid fossils.

Black bear cubs are born in caves. They stay inside until they are a few months old. Find three bear cubs.

Cave salamanders make their homes in damp, dark caves. Can you see eight?

Wheat fields

Wheat is a type of grass that is farmed in many parts of the world. It is a very useful plant.

The grain is ground into flour and the dry stalks, called straw, are used as cattle bedding.

USA

You can find wheat fields like these in Oregon, USA.

Barn swallows fly at high speeds, swooping to catch insects. Find 11.

Tractors pull all kinds of heavy farm machinery. Spot five more.

Bindweed wraps itself around crops and grows very quickly. Find eight bindweed flowers.

Ring-necked pheasants nest on the ground in wheat fields. Spot three.

Hungry white-tailed deer sometimes wander into fields to nibble the wheat. Can you spot one?

Can you see nine monarch butterflies?

Combine harvesters cut down wheat and separate the grain from the straw. Spot two.

Grain is dropped from a combine harvester into a grain trailer. Can you spot three grain trailers?

Baling machines gather up straw and roll it into bales. Spot two bailing machines.

Grasshoppers eat all kinds of plants, including wheat. Find seven.

Spot 12 straw bales.

Farmers use barns to keep cattle in or to store grain or farm machinery. Find three barns.

Young fieldmice climb wheat stalks to collect grain to eat. Can you see six more fieldmice?

Tropical rainforest

In hot, steamy rainforests, some trees grow very tall. Many animals, and even some plants, live high up in the trees because there is more light there than on the ground. This area is called the canopy.

Tamanduas spend most of their time in trees, searching for ants to eat. Spot four.

Golden eyelash vipers slither along branches in the canopy. Find three.

Spot seven more blue morpho butterflies.

Can you find six red-eyed tree frogs?

Central America

Tropical rainforests cover many parts of Central America.

Some orchids grow on trees. Their roots soak up moisture from the air. Find 20 orchid flowers.

Capuchin monkeys use their tails to grab branches as they swing from tree to tree. Spot eight.

Toucans aren't very good at flying. They hop from tree to tree, looking for fruit. Spot five.

Scientists hide in tree houses to study rainforest plants and animals. Can you find two tree houses?

Monkey-ladder vines have thick stems and hang from branches high in the canopy. Can you spot five?

People explore the canopy using treetop walkways. Find three walkways.

Strawberry poison-dart frogs have red and blue skin. This warns attackers that they are poisonous. Find seven more.

A waterfall is a sudden, vertical drop in a river as it plunges over a steep hillside. Spot one.

Tank plants grow in cracks on trees. They trap the water they need inside their tightly packed leaves. Spot four more.

Craggy coast

Coastlines are constantly changing shape. Powerful waves gradually wear away some parts of the cliffs, while in other places, pieces of worn-away rock are washed ashore, forming beaches.

Northern Europe is known for its rugged coastlines.

Wind turbines turn wind energy into electricity. Find eight.

Can you spot 18 herring gulls?

Lighthouses flash to warn ships about dangerous coastlines. Spot one lighthouse.

Atlantic puffins spend most of the year far out at sea. They only come ashore to nest. Find eight more.

A trawler is powered by a motor. This turns a propeller, which pushes the boat forward. Spot four trawlers.

Orcas hunt for fish, squid, sea birds and sharks. Can you spot six?

Spot two hang-gliders soaring on the wind.

Bottlenose dolphins often swim alongside boats. Can you find eight?

Mooring buoys are anchored to the sea bed. People tie their boats to them. Find five mooring buoys.

Seals have a layer of fat under their skin which keeps them warm in icy water. Spot five.

Yachts are pushed through the water by the wind blowing against their sails. Spot ten.

As waves crash against the cliffs, they carve arches out of the rock. Can you see two arches?

A stack is a pillar of rock in the sea. A stack is formed when the middle of an arch collapses. Find five stacks.

245

African grasslands

Grasslands are open areas of land covered in many different types of grasses. Because of the abundance of grasses, they attract plant-eating animals, which in turn attract meat-eaters.

Grasslands like this are found in southern Africa.

Can you spot 12 African elephants?

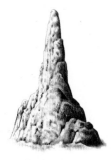

Insects called termites live in mounds, which they build out of mud and saliva. Spot eight termite mounds.

Springboks spring into the air when they are afraid, which is how they got their name. Find 24.

A giraffe's long neck helps it to reach the leaves of acacia trees. Spot ten more giraffes.

Vultures fly over grasslands, searching for dead animals to eat. Spot four vultures.

246

Raised rocky areas called koppies make good resting spots for lions. Find two lions on a koppie.

People watch animals from safari trucks. Spot three trucks.

Masked weaverbirds build onion-shaped nests out of blades of grass. Find four weaverbird nests.

Acacia trees provide food and shelter for zebras, birds and many other animals. Spot eight more acacia trees.

Zebras live in groups, so that some can watch out for predators while others eat, drink or rest. Can you spot 12 zebras?

Animals gather at water holes to drink. Find three water holes.

Warthogs keep cool by wallowing in water holes. Spot seven warthogs.

Cheetahs can run faster than any other animal. Find one.

Winding river

Canada

High up in the mountains, rain and melted snow make streams, which join together to make rivers.

Rivers flow downhill, winding across the land until they flow into a lake or reach the sea.

Rivers like this flow into the Great Lakes in Canada.

Spot five green darner dragonflies.

An oxbow lake forms when a bend in a river becomes cut off from the river. Find one oxbow lake.

Wood ducks tip upside down in the water to feed on water plants. Spot seven.

Painted turtles often sunbathe on logs or rocks. Can you find six more?

Spot two bridges.

Yellow-spotted salamanders vist rivers to lay their eggs. Can you find three salamanders?

Spot two canoes.

Water liles have big leaves that float on the surface of the water. Find 15 water lily leaves.

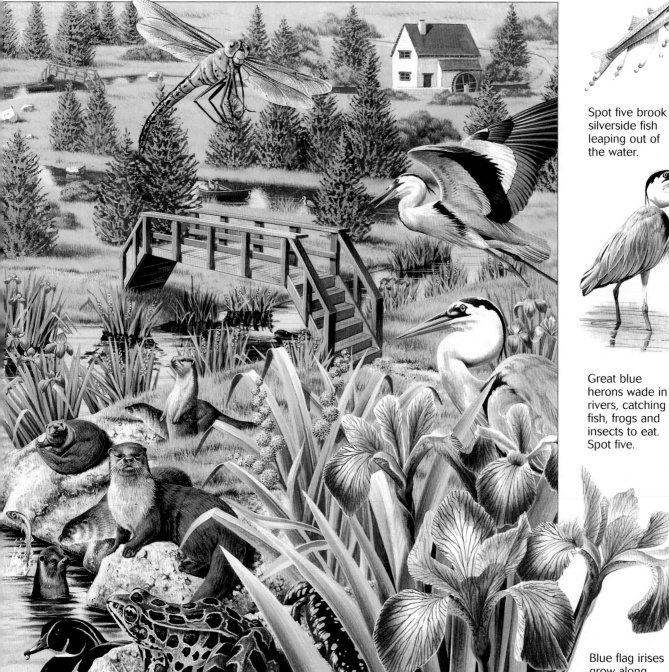

Spot five brook silverside fish leaping out of the water.

Great blue herons wade in rivers, catching fish, frogs and insects to eat. Spot five.

Blue flag irises grow along riverbanks. Can you find 21 more iris flowers?

River otters have sleek, waterproof fur and short, powerful legs to help them swim. Find ten.

At a water mill, the river turns a wheel, which powers a machine that grinds grain into flour. Find one water mill.

Hot spots

Beneath the surface of the Earth, there is a mass of hot, liquid rock. In volcanic areas, this can seep up through the ground, causing volcanoes and other dramatic natural features.

New Zealand is well-known for its volcanic areas.

Mud volcanoes are small, cone-shaped mounds that ooze mud, clay and volcanic gases. Can you find three?

Can you find five New Zealand wood pigeons?

Hot springs are found in volcanic areas. Minerals turn the water bright orange and green. Find three hot springs.

New Zealand falcons live in pine forests near the hot springs. Spot two.

Mud pots are bubbling pools of runny mud. The bubbles are gases escaping from underground. Find four mud pots.

Sometimes, when the sun shines through steam spurting from a geyser, a rainbow forms. Spot one rainbow.

Can you find five tourists taking photographs?

A geyser is a jet of hot water and steam that shoots into the air from a hole in the ground. Spot one more geyser.

You can see a dramatic view of the volcanic landscape from a helicopter. Spot two helicopters.

Volcanic gases from deep under the ground escape through vents called fumaroles. Spot 12 fumaroles.

New Zealand's rugged terrain is ideal for mountain biking. Spot four cyclists.

Planet Earth answers

The keys on the next few pages show you exactly where to find all the animals, plants and other things in the big scenes in the last part of this book. You can use these keys to check your answers, or to help you if you have a problem finding anything.

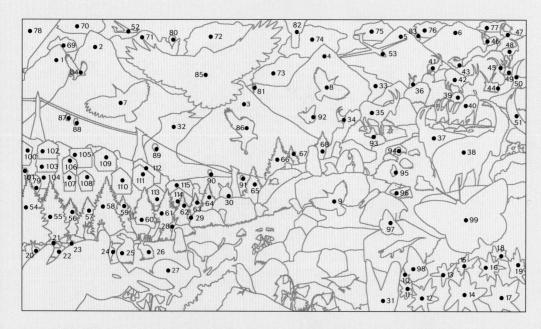

Alpine slopes 230–231

Snowy peaks, 1, 2, 3, 4, 5, 6
Wallcreepers, 7, 8, 9
Edelweiss flowers, 10, 11, 12, 13, 14, 15, 16, 17, 18, 19
Alpine hares, 20, 21, 22, 23, 24, 25, 26, 27, 28, 29, 30, 31
Glaciers, 32, 33
Alpine ibexes, 34, 35, 36, 37, 38, 39, 40, 41, 42, 43, 44, 45, 46, 47, 48, 49, 50, 51
Gliders, 52, 53
Spruce trees, 54, 55, 56, 57, 58, 59, 60, 61, 62, 63, 64, 65, 66, 67, 68
Cumulus clouds, 69, 70, 71, 72, 73, 74, 75, 76, 77
Hot-air balloons, 78, 79, 80, 81, 82, 83
Golden eagles, 84, 85, 86
Cable cars, 87, 88, 89, 90, 91
Purple-shot copper butterflies, 92, 93, 94, 95, 96, 97, 98, 99
Chalets, 100, 101, 102, 103, 104, 105, 106, 107, 108, 109, 110, 111, 112, 113, 114, 115

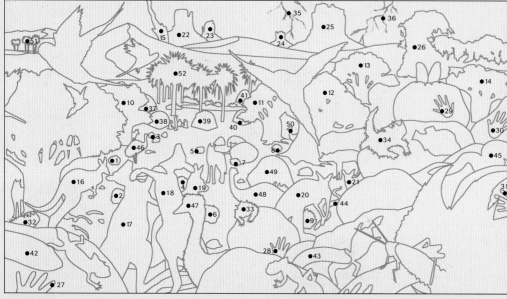

Australian desert 232–233

Tumbleweed plants, 1, 2, 3, 4, 5, 6, 7, 8, 9
Baobab trees, 10, 11, 12, 13, 14
Dust devil, 15
Kangaroos, 16, 17, 18, 19, 20, 21
Mesas, 22, 23, 24, 25
Bushfire, 26
Hand prints, 27, 28, 29, 30, 31
Thorny devils, 32, 33, 34
Bolts of lightning, 35, 36
Tents, 37, 38, 39, 40, 41
Woma pythons, 42, 43, 44, 45
Emus, 46, 47, 48, 49, 50
Oases, 51, 52

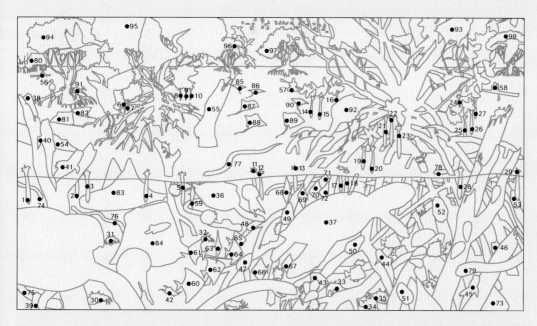

Mangrove swamp 234–235

Mangrove seedlings, 1, 2, 3, 4, 5, 6, 7, 8, 9, 10, 11, 12, 13, 14, 15, 16, 17, 18, 19, 20, 21, 22, 23, 24, 25, 26, 27, 28, 29

Male fiddler crabs, 30, 31, 32, 33, 34, 35

Hawksbill turtles, 36, 37

Mudskippers, 38, 39, 40, 41, 42, 43, 44, 45, 46

Oysters, 47, 48, 49, 50, 51, 52, 53

Saltwater crocodiles, 54, 55

Kayaks, 56, 57, 58

Silver moony fish, 59, 60, 61, 62, 63, 64, 65, 66, 67, 68, 69, 70, 71, 72, 73

Banded sea kraits, 74, 75, 76, 77, 78, 79

Hut on stilts, 80

Cownose rays, 81, 82, 83, 84, 85, 86, 87, 88, 89, 90

Little egrets, 91, 92, 93

Mangrove trees, 94, 95, 96, 97, 98

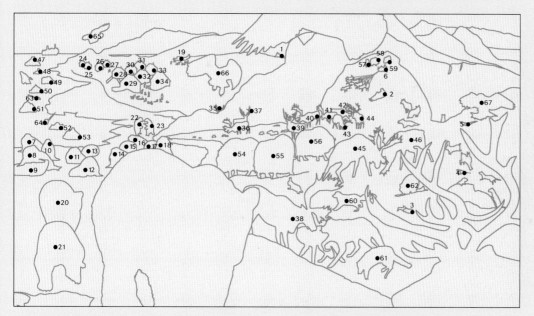

Icy Arctic 236–237

Snowmobiles, 1, 2

Lemmings, 3, 4, 5

Sled pulled by husky dogs, 6

Walruses, 7, 8, 9, 10, 11, 12, 13, 14, 15, 16, 17, 18

Cargo plane, 19

Polar bears, 20, 21, 22, 23

Houses, 24, 25, 26, 27, 28, 29, 30, 31, 32, 33, 34

Caribou, 35, 36, 37, 38, 39, 40, 41, 42, 43, 44, 45, 46

Icebergs, 47, 48, 49, 50, 51, 52, 53

Musk oxen, 54, 55, 56, 57, 58, 59

Arctic foxes, 60, 61, 62

Narwhals, 63, 64

Snowy owls, 65, 66, 67

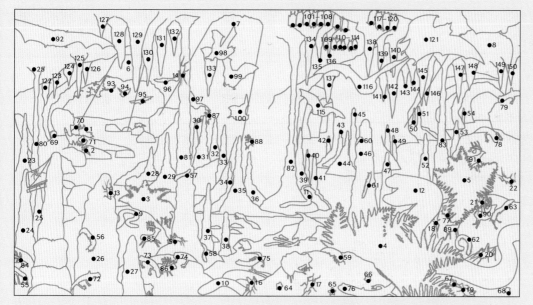

Limestone cave 238–239

Ferns, 1, 2, 3, 4, 5

Sink-holes, 6, 7, 8

Rat snakes, 9, 10, 11, 12

Cave crickets, 13, 14, 15, 16, 17, 18, 19, 20, 21, 22

Stalagmites, 23, 24, 25, 26, 27, 28, 29, 30, 31, 32, 33, 34, 35, 36, 37, 38, 39, 40, 41, 42, 43, 44, 45, 46, 47, 48, 49, 50, 51, 52, 53, 54

Giant millipedes, 55, 56, 57, 58, 59, 60, 61, 62, 63

Fossils, 64, 65, 66, 67, 68

Black bear cubs, 69, 70, 71

Cave salamanders, 72, 73, 74, 75, 76, 77, 78, 79

Columns, 80, 81, 82, 83

Deer pictures, 84, 85, 86, 87, 88, 89, 90, 91

Little brown bats, 92, 93, 94, 95, 96, 97, 98, 99, 100, 101, 102, 103, 104, 105, 106, 107, 108, 109, 110, 111, 112, 113, 114, 115, 116, 117, 118, 119, 120, 121

Stalactites, 122, 123, 124, 125, 126, 127, 128, 129, 130, 131, 132, 133, 134, 135, 136, 137, 138, 139, 140, 141, 142, 143, 144, 145, 146, 147, 148, 149, 150

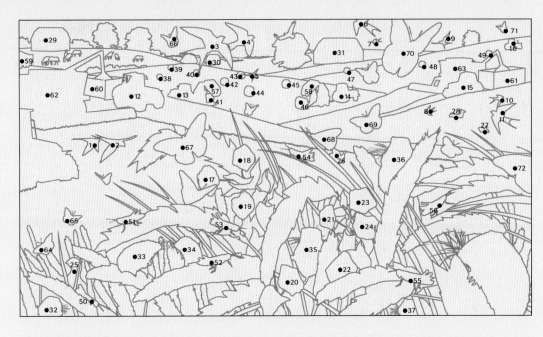

Wheat fields 240–241

Barn swallows, 1, 2, 3, 4, 5, 6, 7, 8, 9, 10, 11
Tractors, 12, 13, 14, 15, 16
Bindweed flowers, 17, 18, 19, 20, 21, 22, 23, 24
Ring-necked pheasants, 25, 26, 27
White-tailed deer, 28
Barns, 29, 30, 31
Fieldmice, 32, 33, 34, 35, 36, 37
Straw bales, 38, 39, 40, 41, 42, 43, 44, 45, 46, 47, 48, 49
Grasshoppers, 50, 51, 52, 53, 54, 55, 56
Baling machines, 57, 58
Grain trailers, 59, 60, 61
Combine harvesters, 62, 63
Monarch butterflies, 64, 65, 66, 67, 68, 69, 70, 71, 72

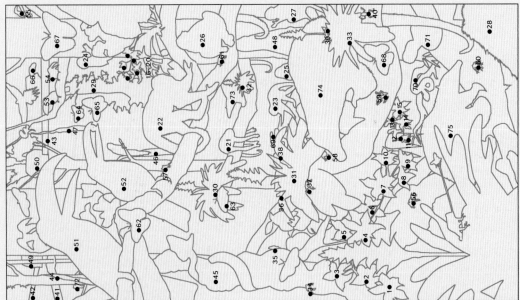

Tropical rainforest 242–243

Orchid flowers, 1, 2, 3, 4, 5, 6, 7, 8, 9, 10, 11, 12, 13, 14, 15, 16, 17, 18, 19, 20
Capuchin monkeys, 21, 22, 23, 24, 25, 26, 27, 28
Waterfall, 29
Tank plants, 30, 31, 32, 33
Strawberry poison-dart frogs, 34, 35, 36, 37, 38, 39, 40
Walkways, 41, 42, 43
Monkey-ladder vines, 44, 45, 46, 47, 48
Tree houses, 49, 50
Toucans, 51, 52, 53, 54, 55
Red-eyed tree frogs, 56, 57, 58, 59, 60, 61
Blue morpho butterflies, 62, 63, 64, 65, 66, 67, 68
Golden eyelash vipers, 69, 70, 71
Tamanduas, 72, 73, 74, 75

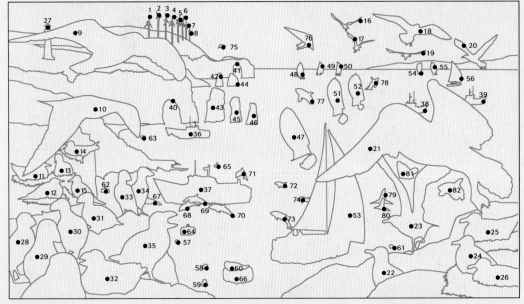

Craggy coast 244–245

Wind turbines, 1, 2, 3, 4, 5, 6, 7, 8
Herring gulls, 9, 10, 11, 12, 13, 14, 15, 16, 17, 18, 19, 20, 21, 22, 23, 24, 25, 26
Lighthouse, 27
Atlantic puffins, 28, 29, 30, 31, 32, 33, 34, 35
Trawlers, 36, 37, 38, 39
Arches, 40, 41
Stacks, 42, 43, 44, 45, 46
Yachts, 47, 48, 49, 50, 51, 52, 53, 54, 55, 56
Seals, 57, 58, 59, 60, 61
Mooring buoys, 62, 63, 64, 65, 66
Bottlenose dolphins, 67, 68, 69, 70, 71, 72, 73, 74
Hang-gliders, 75, 76
Orcas (killer whales), 77, 78, 79, 80, 81, 82

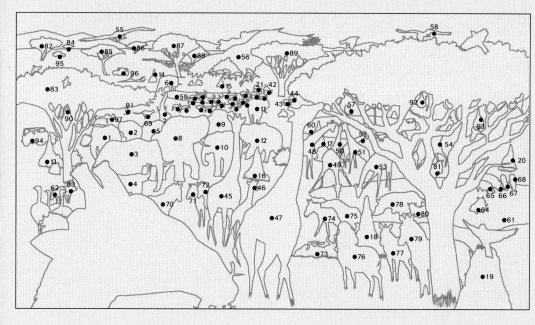

African grasslands 246–247

African elephants, 1, 2, 3, 4, 5, 6, 7, 8, 9, 10, 11, 12

Termite mounds, 13, 14, 15, 16, 17, 18, 19, 20

Springboks, 21, 22, 23, 24, 25, 26, 27, 28, 29, 30, 31, 32, 33, 34, 35, 36, 37, 38, 39, 40, 41, 42, 43, 44

Giraffes, 45, 46, 47, 48, 49, 50, 51, 52, 53, 54

Vultures, 55, 56, 57, 58

Water holes, 59, 60, 61

Warthogs, 62, 63, 64, 65, 66, 67, 68

Cheetah, 69

Zebras, 70, 71, 72, 73, 74, 75, 76, 77, 78, 79, 80, 81

Acacia trees, 82, 83, 84, 85, 86, 87, 88, 89

Weaverbird nests, 90, 91, 92, 93

Safari trucks, 94, 95, 96

Lions on a koppie, 97

Winding river 248–249

Green darner dragonflies, 1, 2, 3, 4, 5

Oxbow lake, 6

Wood ducks, 7, 8, 9, 10, 11, 12, 13

Painted turtles, 14, 15, 16, 17, 18, 19

Bridges, 20, 21

River otters, 22, 23, 24, 25, 26, 27, 28, 29, 30, 31

Water mill, 32

Blue flag iris flowers, 33, 34, 35, 36, 37, 38, 39, 40, 41, 42, 43, 44, 45, 46, 47, 48, 49, 50, 51, 52, 53

Great blue herons, 54, 55, 56, 57, 58

Brook silverside fish, 59, 60, 61, 62, 63

Water lily leaves, 64, 65, 66, 67, 68, 69, 70, 71, 72, 73, 74, 75, 76, 77, 78

Canoes, 79, 80

Yellow-spotted salamanders, 81, 82, 83

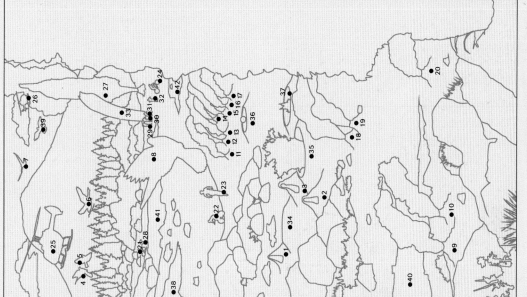

Hot spots 250–251

Mud volcanoes, 1, 2, 3

New Zealand wood pigeons, 4, 5, 6, 7, 8

Fumaroles, 9, 10, 11, 12, 13, 14, 15, 16, 17, 18, 19, 20

Cyclists, 21, 22, 23, 24

Helicopters, 25, 26

Geyser, 27

Tourists taking photographs, 28, 29, 30, 31, 32

Rainbow, 33

Mud pots, 34, 35, 36, 37

New Zealand falcons, 38, 39

Hot springs, 40, 41, 42

Acknowledgements

Part One: The Dinosaur Search

Written by	Rosie Heywood
Illustrated by	Studio Galante and Inklink Firenze
Designed by	Mary Cartwright
Edited by	Philippa Wingate

Part Two: The History Search

Written by	Kamini Khanduri
Illustrated by	David Hancock
Designed by	Ian Cleaver
Edited by	Felicity Brooks

Part Three: The Animal Search

Written by	Caroline Young
Illustrated by	Ian Jackson
Designed by	Andy Dixon
Edited by	Felicity Brooks

Part Four: The Castle Search

Written by	Jane Bingham
Illustrated by	Dominic Groebner
Designed by	Stephen Wright
Edited by	Jane Chisholm

Part Five: The Undersea Search

Written by	Kate Needham
Illustrated by	Ian Jackson
Designed by	Andy Griffin
Edited by	Felicity brooks

Part Six: The Bug Search

Written by	Caroline Young
Illustrated by	Ian Jackson
Designed by	Andy Dixon
Edited by	Kamini Khanduri

Part Seven: Planet Earth Search

Written by	Emma Helbrough
Illustrated by	Ian Jackson
Designed by	Stephen Wright
Edited by	Anna Milbourne

Geography consultant:	Dr. Roger Trend
Scientific consultants:	Dr. John Bevan
	Dr. David Duthie
	Dr. David Norman
	Dr. John Rostron
	Dr. Margaret Rostron
History consultants:	Dr. Anne Millard
	Dr. Abigail Wheatley
Cartographic consultant:	Craig Asquith
Diving consultant:	Reg Vallintine
Keys illustrator:	Edwina Hannam
Additional editing:	Natalie Abi-Ezzi
	Ben Denne
	Gillian Doherty
	Rosie Heywood
	Claire Masset
	Fiona Patchett
	Rachael Swann
	Sophy Tahta
Additional design:	Will Dawes
	Katarina Dragoslavic
	Natacha Goransky
	Stephanie Jones
	Rebecca Mills
	Lindsay North
	Mike Olley
	Susannah Owen
	Kerry Pearson
	John Russell

With thanks to:

Mr Fred Redding, Company Archivist, Selfridges, London, UK; The Archive Departments at Harrods Ltd. and John Lewis Partnership, UK; Saki Daorana, Qaanaaq Tourist Office, Greenland; Katrina Knill, Dept. of Conservation, New Zealand; Darren Naish, School of Earth and Environmental Sciences, University of Portsmouth, UK.